C000224749

Hans Erik Östlund was born
graduate of The Stockholm School of Economics. He has
had a professional career in investment banking between
London and South America; and has lived in Argentina,
Brazil, Chile, and Peru. He currently resides with his family
in Lima, Peru. *Babies from Ukraine* is his third novel.

To my wife, Zelma, and my friend, Emily

Hans Erik Östlund

BABIES FROM UKRAINE

AUSTIN MACAULEY PUBLISHERS™

LONDON • CAMBRIDGE • NEW YORK • SHARJAH

A CIP catalogue record for this title is available from the British Library.

ISBN 9781398475212 (Paperback)
ISBN 9781398475229 (ePub e-book)

www.austinmacauley.com

First Published 2022
Austin Macauley Publishers Ltd®
1 Canada Square
Canary Wharf
London
E14 5AA

Chapter I

When Alicia's mid-morning café-latte arrived at her table, she smiled happily at the waitress, who was unused to overly polite customers (especially in the morning). Alicia received a large, toothy smile in return. Spread out on the table in front of her were two magazines, *Fit Pregnancy,* and *American Baby.* An article entitled 'Old and Pregnant' had just caught her eye, and within seconds she was engrossed in the multiple horrors a woman who is expecting and over forty should prepare herself for:

"The risk for both mother and child increases after the age of thirty-five, particularly if it's the first pregnancy. The risk of Down Syndrome increases to one in one hundred, but there are other risks involved as well, including gestational diabetes, pre-eclampsia, miscarriage, pre-term delivery, problems involving the placenta, etc. However, the chance of stillbirth is very small indeed, and there is no proven link that associates autism with mature pregnancy."

As Alicia looked up, a sigh escaped her lips. She quickly finished her coffee, packed the magazines away, and exited the café. Pulling the collar of her wool coat up to her neck, she set out at a brisk pace. She was on her way to the offices of Bowen & Hughes, where she worked under the slightly inflated title of head of corporate affairs. The position demanded an office rather than the cubicle she currently occupied but that was only a temporary inconvenience while she was negotiating her terms and conditions. She hadn't been keen on the plain old head of research and compliance title and had successfully argued that research and compliance could be interpreted as corporate affairs. The idea had really belonged to her good friend Eric Holstein, who always encouraged her to reach out and grab her dreams with both hands. Without Eric's support, Alicia would have never dared to suggest the title change in the first place.

She checked with Annette, the office receptionist, and Alicia's very unofficial secretary, and was pleased to discover that she had no meetings scheduled for the day except for a doctor's appointment later that afternoon. Therefore, she went through the previous month's billings and had a sandwich and a coke delivered to her desk for lunch. By working through her break, she felt less guilty about arranging drinks with her friend Elisabeth after her visit to her doctor.

She liked her doctor and had been his patient for many years. He was about ten years her senior but very up to date with modern medical trends. She trusted him.

After listening to Alicia, Dr Ross Gordon suggested that, given the risks involved, she and her fiancé Adrian should consider adoption instead. "There are so many babies born into this world whose biological parents are unfit or unwilling to care for them," he added.

"But a pregnancy is something so special," Alicia protested weakly.

Dr Gordon seemed to ignore Alicia's protests and continued. "Furthermore, you need to consider the possibility that you could bleed continuously throughout the pregnancy, which would result in spending most of your gestation in bed. It is very unlikely that you will be able to fulfil your work duties while you are expecting."

Alicia promised her doctor she would discuss adoption with Adrian, who was both romantic and practical. But first, she was going to discuss the issue with Elisabeth, even though she already knew what her friend's position would be.

Elisabeth had arrived at the Hotel Metro rooftop bar first and was already seated at a tall circular table when Alicia arrived. They hugged and kissed with genuine affection. Elisabeth was having a martini. Alicia guessed the cocktail was made with gin instead of vodka, as it was her friend's new favourite drink. She decided against the potent concoction and asked for a neat Jameson instead.

"You and your proud Irish heritage," Elisabeth said matter-of-factly. "So, you wanted to see me?" She paused before continuing. "I thought you sounded a little bit…excited, my love." Alicia took out the two magazines from her bag and put them in front of Elisabeth. "Don't tell me, you're pregnant!" Elisabeth gasped.

"No, not yet. I'm just considering what it would be like to have a child," Alicia said in a soft voice.

"Ah, but of course. Baby Syndrome," Elisabeth said. "I've been waiting for this but please don't consider me an option for babysitting," she added with a crooked grin.

Elisabeth and her husband James were both in their fifties and had never had children. Alicia thought that was a bit of a shame, especially since they were such a lovely couple. They were also extremely loaded and would have therefore been able to give a child a wonderful start in life.

9

"Well, I'm no spring chicken, so my doctor has just given me a lecture on the unwanted children who need foster and adoptive parents." Alicia sighed and then sheepishly looked up at her friend for support.

"*If* it's children you want, that sounds very sensible to me," Elisabeth exclaimed, heavily emphasising her first word.

"Well, it's just that…I think Adrian would make a very good father. And, if I'm honest, I can absolutely see myself raising an independent little creature." Alicia finished with a dreamy smile. *And I'll make a much better mom than my own mother,* she thought. It was no secret that she didn't get along with her mother. And if she included her sister into the mix, the three of them didn't get along. Her father was a different matter; she adored him. She knew that Adrian would be just like him once they had their own child.

"Well, you know my opinion on babies, so I'm probably not the best person to consult with. Before deciding, however, I think you should also consider hiring a nanny because of your career. So, it *is* a big decision." As usual, Elisabeth didn't hold back and said exactly what she thought. "Now that we have exhausted that subject, let's talk about this coming weekend. I would love to have dinner on Saturday at Rafael, and brunch on Sunday at the Lighthouse…Persuade Adrian, will you, my love?" Elisabeth was almost pleading.

"Sounds great," Alicia replied. "As far as I'm aware, we have no prior commitments."

They ordered another round of the same drinks and returned to small talk. Alicia always felt so comfortable in the company of her older friend but even still she couldn't shake the idea that declining late afternoon drinks – either because

she was pregnant or had to be home to tend to her little one –
would irk Elisabeth.

Alicia let her mind wander and she pictured Adrian,
herself, and a gorgeous little chubby-faced toddler. They were
walking hand in hand in autumnal Central Park; a beautiful
and happy family chasing golden-brown leaves together.
Alicia couldn't wait to be a mother. No matter what anyone
said, she was determined that a child would be a part of her
future, and soon. She yearned for it.

Chapter II

While Alicia was having drinks with Elisabeth, her fiancé was attending a meeting at NYU, where he was a professor of economics. He and his co-workers were planning the postgraduate and PHD classes for the next semester. Adrian had the tall, dark, and handsome looks of the hero in romantic novels. He also had the charm and good manners of a true gentleman. This, combined with his highly esteemed career and healthy bank account balance, made Adrian a catch in almost any woman's eyes.

The constant giggling and eyelash fluttering from the women around him had been mildly annoying for Alicia but now it made her anxious instead of irritated. A few months earlier, a woman obsessed with Adrian had kidnapped and stabbed Alicia. In doing so, Marion had caused Alicia to lose a kidney as well as her unborn child. Alicia now saw harmless flirting as sinister and calculating. She and Adrian had argued several times in the past few weeks over her insecurities. Adrian understood Alicia's paranoia but he hated how badly the incident had affected her confidence. He made a point of ignoring flirty women. However, he couldn't ignore everyone, and that's when the arguments started.

Looking up, he realised that his colleagues were wrapping up. He had missed a lot of the conversation. "Helen, could you please send me a copy of the programmes we've discussed today?"

Helen was blonde and in her early thirties. She worked as the general office assistant and was very friendly, and only slightly flirty. In the past, Adrian had laughed and joked with her but he now kept their conversations short and only about work. He knew he shouldn't change the way he spoke to women, but Marion had not been a one-off; Alicia had also been kidnapped by a bent cop only a few months prior to Marion stabbing her. Adrian didn't want Alicia to experience any more pain, but he realised he needed to stop pandering to her insecurities. He worried they were falling into an unhealthy pattern, which could lead to disaster in their relationship.

As he was leaving the meeting, Adrian glanced down at his phone and noticed that he had missed a call from Alicia. He called her back and instantly noticed the background noise. "Where are you, Darling?" he asked curiously.

"I'm at Hotel Metro with Elisabeth, and she's asking if we can have dinner with them at Rafael's on Saturday and brunch at the Lighthouse on Sunday. She said all of us need a good catch-up. Please say yes…" Adrian heard Alicia whine, but he couldn't see the funny face she was making at Elisabeth. "OK, that's settled then!" Alicia said before giving him the chance to respond. "And I'll do the cooking tonight," she added.

Adrian knew that Alicia felt guilty for forcing his hand, and he knew she was giving Elisabeth a thumbs-up. "No, I'll cook tonight. How about a rack of lamb?" He knew she loved the way he cooked lamb.

"Oh, that sounds wonderful," she said with an audible sigh of relief. "Do you need me to buy anything on my way home?"

Adrian stifled a chuckle and said, "Yes, carrots would be good."

"Yep, I know. The small ones, right?" Alicia asked.

"Yep, you're right. I gotta go, babe. Love you."

Adrian hung up before she heard him laugh. He was making his way through the NYU corridors with a huge grin plastered on his face while Alicia was explaining to Elisabeth that they were all set for the weekend ahead. "And Adrian is going to cook his famous rack of lamb tonight."

"Sounds good! I might just tag along."

"Sorry, no tagging along," Alicia said. She went on to explain that Adrian always cut out each cutlet and wrapped the tip of every bone in aluminium foil so they could eat them in bed while watching Netflix.

"What are *the small ones*?" Elisabeth asked.

"Oh, they're carrots," Alicia explained. "Adrian likes those tiny ones. He boils them in water, and then he adds salt, sugar, and lemon. He leaves enough of the stalks so that we can eat them by hand as well. We dip them in fresh mint sauce. It's delicious."

"Gosh, sounds like the little pots of baby food!" Elisabeth was being critical instead of sarcastic, but Alicia decided to ignore her friend and asked their server for the cheque. The two women promptly took the elevator down from the fourteenth-floor bar to the ground floor. When they got there, they hugged and kissed goodnight.

Chapter III

Adrian ended the call with Alicia; it was good to hear her sounding bright and breezy once again. He hadn't realised how much he had missed her laugh until just a moment ago when that husky sound caused his heart to do its familiar little tell-tale dance in his chest. It had been a while since he'd last had that feeling.

He sighed and raked his hand through his hair. Although he wasn't hot, he felt grubby and was looking forward to a hot shower. He wondered why his steps felt heavier than usual, especially since hearing Alicia laugh. In an attempt to wake himself up a little, he half-heartedly tried to sprint. He failed and fell into an awkward jog instead. He wondered if all of this was about Alicia's insecurity, or perhaps his own. He suddenly stopped walking as his thoughts shifted into defensive mode. He wondered if Alicia was, in fact, just another jealous female, he had certainly had his fair share of that type. But no, he knew Alicia wasn't really like that, she was well above being jealous. Perhaps it did indeed have something to do with him. Maybe it was his behaviour toward the opposite sex? *But I love them, no, I love Alicia,* he corrected himself midway through his thought. What was it that his best pal from his college years had called him? *The chick magnet.* Yes, that was it. He smiled as he remembered those days. *That was then but now…What about now?* He questioned himself in earnest.

As Adrian stumbled through his thoughts, a blonde student passed him and caught his eye. *Her ass is pear-shaped,* he reflected. *Not nicely round but pear-shaped. Alicia is slimmer and maybe a bit bonier but it's her ass I really want to grab now.* He shook his head and clutched his upper body by wrapping his arms around himself. *Be real,* he cautioned himself. *Alicia not only deserves my respect but also my unconditional love. She is a young yet experienced woman who is by my side. I will never let her down. I truly love her above all others.*

He released himself and managed a few steps forward. But now, totally consumed by his thoughts of Alicia, he started to reflect on how they had first met in Arequipa, *La Ciudad Blanca*, in southern Peru. He had thought the older couple travelling with her had been her parents, and he chuckled again at the thought. Their romance had lasted beyond the vacation, and it had also survived some individuals' very sinister attempts at ending Alicia's life. As if that hadn't been enough to test them, they then combined two apartments in his building, arranging the perfect yin and yang style of living.

Suddenly, Adrian felt much lighter of heart. He started walking again, and his footsteps had a spring to them that they didn't have a moment ago. He knew what to do. He was going to treat his lady to the best lamb chops ever. He had already prepared the same dinner for her several times before, but it was her favourite. He stopped once again, deciding the two of them had reached the point in their relationship that called for him to employ attentive listening and thoughtful replies.

"Sometimes, life calls for more than just shortcuts and simple solutions," he whispered to himself as he hurried along at a marching pace. Suddenly, he couldn't wait to get home and, more importantly, to Alicia.

Chapter IV

Yonkers, with a population of just over two hundred thousand, ranks fourth in New York State after New York City, Buffalo, and Rochester. It borders New York City's borough of the Bronx and is situated on hilly terrain, which radiates out from the eastern bank of the Hudson River to a height of just over four hundred feet. Yonkers' main attraction is the Hudson River Museum, but it is also well known for its *racino*, Empire, which hosts video slot machines for racing and gambling. The main street is Central Park Avenue, known to locals simply as Central Avenue. Situated on Central Avenue is a small adoption agency called Tomorrow that employs only two people, Roland Thompson and his assistant/secretary/receptionist, Betsy Borne.

The interior of the Tomorrow Adoption Agency is relatively sleek and decorated contemporarily. This was largely due to Betsy, who had suggested that anything to do with babies and small children should be arranged neatly and demonstrate cleanliness. The reception area, which was Betsy's domain, housed a modern leather sofa that was large and bright red. Two adjacent steel chairs with beige leather upholstery complemented the smart-looking statement piece. To Betsy's right was a small meeting room with an oval-shaped glass table and six chairs of the same beige leather and steel frames. On the glass table was a display of magazines about babies, plus one copy of *The New York Times*. Roland's small office was situated to the left of the reception area.

Roland was sitting in his office, preparing a speech for a conference on adoption that he would attend the following week. Roland was a man in his early forties who liked to dress well, and today he was wearing a navy-blue jacket, olive green trousers, and a white shirt with a brown silk tie to match his formal Florsheim shoes. He was of average build with a serious face under dark brown hair. His eyes were also brown but neither dark nor pale, just a sludge brown. He was due to visit some clients in Manhattan, so he asked Betsy to get him a taxi to take him to the station at White Plains. There, he would board the commuter train and ride to Grand Central.

Roland was a bachelor and wished to neither reproduce a child nor adopt one. Regardless, he knew he would probably never qualify anyway. The screening process that enabled people to qualify for adoption had become exceedingly difficult to pass and very bureaucratic. Very few applicants managed to meet the strict criteria, this allowed people like himself to earn a very decent wage by holding the hands of prospective parents through the lengthy process. Like any other market, the forces of supply and demand needed to be met, and this increasingly led to less orthodox methods including outright illegal adoptions. This was the very subject of the speech he was working on. However, today was the allotted day he had arranged for collecting fees from the clients he had successfully arranged adoptions for. Although fees were payable throughout the whole process, Roland preferred to collect the larger fees from successful adoptions in person. He made the excuse that his responsibilities included visiting the child's new home, but the truth was that he wanted to make sure he got his big fat cheque immediately.

Roland boarded the train, found a seat, and retrieved a list of three addresses from his inside pocket. A sly grin appeared on his thin lips. He took comfort in knowing he would return later with three cheques totalling eighteen thousand dollars.

Chapter V

Alicia and Adrian huddled cosily together in bed. Both were wearing their pyjamas and watching a movie on Netflix. On a tray that had been placed between them was a large plate of perfectly cooked lamb cutlets, the tiny carrots Alicia had purchased on her way home, and a small bowl of freshly made mint sauce. A bottle of strong but delicious Chianti wine had been placed on Adrian's bedside table.

Alicia was reflecting on the fact that they were so happy and so right together. A night snuggled up to Adrian was perfect and much preferred over a night out at a posh restaurant. Not that she didn't love going out; she just loved the intimacy of their nights cuddled up in bed together.

Alicia turned to Adrian suddenly and asked him to pause the movie. There was something she wanted to discuss with him, and she was ready now. As always, he had the remote control, which seemed to be attached to his hand. Alicia thought that removing the remote from her man's hand was akin to cutting off one of his most precious organs.

"Darling, I visited my doctor today," Alicia said softly.

"Tell me!" Adrian tossed the remote to the edge of the bed and turned to Alicia, reaching for her hand, and giving her his undivided attention. There was anticipation in his voice, but also a small dose of fear.

"Well, we discussed pregnancy...Although he didn't say it in so many words, I got the feeling that he is in favour of us adopting rather than tackling the risks involved with pregnancy at my age. And of course, there are the injuries I sustained when Marion...when she did what she did." Alicia didn't like talking about the attack but this was due to what she had lost, rather than the injuries she had sustained.

"Well, we can't really argue with him. He's the expert after all." Adrian paused for a moment and then continued in a softer voice. "Although adopting means you'll never get to experience pregnancy. If that's fine with you, then it's fine by me." He continued holding her hand in his as he spoke.

"The truth is I would love to carry our baby. I'm sure it would be glorious, but I also understand that it could be a nightmare. What if something were to happen to our baby? You know I would never forgive myself. And I'm not sure I could go through the loss of another one." Alicia spoke with a hint of reluctance but was being completely honest.

"We need to be positive about this, and without any regrets. If we can't, well, I think we should wait a while," Adrian said with equal honesty.

"But Darling, I really want a baby now, while we're still young. And I think you'll be such a good father, I really do!" Alicia heard the vibration of unshed tears in her voice.

Adrian also heard her voice break and reassured her gently. "Alicia, you'll be the best mother any child could ever wish for."

They both realised that they were back onto more positive ground and said, almost in tandem, "Let's go for it!" Both automatically reached for their wine glasses and toasted.

"Cheers, my beautiful girl," Adrian said. "But which of the two plans are we celebrating?" he added innocently.

"Our decision to adopt," Alicia said firmly. "At least that's what I'm going to start investigating as of tomorrow, as long as you don't think it's too early?"

"The sooner the better, I say!" Adrian replied with absolute conviction. He wanted Alicia to know that he wanted this just as much as she did.

"Do you want the rest of my wine? I'm going to pour myself a whiskey." Alicia got up from the bed and made her way to the living room. "Be right back," she called out in a considerably lighter tone.

When she returned with her drink, they realised they had both lost interest in the movie and decided to finish it another day. They started talking excitedly about what adoption would mean for them. They quickly came to the conclusion that their chances would probably increase if they were married as opposed to their current arrangement. They eventually fell asleep holding hands, both content and happy with their decision.

Chapter VI

Kyiv, the capital of Ukraine, has a population of nearly three million people. The city boasts a long and colourful history full of heroic deeds. These deeds, which were accomplished over many centuries, earned Kyiv its name, *the mother of Slavic cities.* It is a fitting title for a city so rich in culture and history. Kyiv's golden era was in the eleventh and twelfth centuries when Kievan Rus was a very rich and powerful federation. It was conveniently located at the centre of the trading routes between the Baltic and Mediterranean seas. The city eventually lost its esteem and was pillaged but Kyiv survived and still amazes many visitors with its sublime beauty.

According to the ancient legends, four siblings founded Kyiv on the eve of the fifth century: brothers Kyi, Scheck, and Khoryv, and their sister, Lybed. The city was named after the eldest brother. Kyiv is the official Ukrainian spelling and means *the city of Kyi. Kiev* is the Russian spelling and recognised worldwide since Soviet times.

Many ancient tribes gathered and settled in and around Kyiv. By the end of the ninth century, the city had become the political and cultural centre of Eastern Slavs. The Great Prince Vladimir introduced Christianity in the year 988, and it quickly became the official religion. This helped establish political and cultural relations with the Byzantium Empire and Bulgaria. Almost fifty thousand people lived in the city at that time, and there were around four hundred churches and eight markets.

Kyiv, which is situated on the Dnieper River, possesses architectural monuments that have been declared world treasures. It is the largest city as well as the cultural, scientific, and industrial centre of Ukraine. It is a place of religious pilgrimage and a very attractive tourist destination.

Few cities in the world boast as many coffee shops as Kyiv and the inhabitants of this majestic and picturesque city love this drink. Coffee was brought to the city by a Ukrainian Cusack from neighbouring Austria. It became the favoured drink, which propelled the growth of thousands of outdoor cafés.

Pavlov Andreiko was in one of the said local outdoor cafés, sitting on a wooden folding chair under a dark yellow awning with his back facing the establishment's open windows. He was enjoying his coffee and brandy, which were accompanied by a fine cigar. The establishment didn't have a liquor license but still stored one of Pavlov's bottles of the finest aged brandy, stashed illegally and inconspicuously under the counter indoors for his personal consumption. Placed on the table before Pavlov was his ledger with coded entries and numbers. His smile indicated that he was a happy man, and his contentment was certainly justified; the papers showed he was well on his way to becoming a billionaire. He was a self-made man in his early sixties, and he certainly didn't feel shy about his success. With a very large fortune and a general lack of scruples, Pavlov contemplated what the evening had in store for him. He decided that a fine supper with his lovely wife – who was in her thirties and half his age

– would be a good start. He contemplated passing the rest of the evening at his favourite and very luxurious brothel.

Pavlov owned one of the largest sex trafficking operations in the world. It was connected to the Russian mafia which controlled much of the world of prostitution. *A man should enjoy his work*, he mused with a wicked grin on his craggy face as he puffed on his Romeo and Julieta cigar. There had been a time when he had only smoked the finest cigars made by Zino Davidoff, an industrious man who had fled Kyiv after the Second World War to set up his world-famous cigar business in Switzerland. However, when the Davidoff brand switched from Cuban tobacco to Central American tobacco in the late sixties, Pavlov decided to change his brand. He found the sweetness of the Cuban wrapper to be exquisite.

His peace of mind was rudely interrupted by the shrill tone of his mobile phone. The call was from his personal assistant, Sofia Dudyk. She had called to inform him that Igor Kovalenko was in town and wanted to see him. Despite the warm August afternoon, Pavlov felt a chill spiral down his spine; that son-of-a-bitch had to be dealt with as a matter of urgency. An evening of wonderful food followed by glorious debauchery was now something he could no longer look forward to. So, he did what he always did in a situation like this and immediately called his wife, Yuliya.

Yuliya answered brusquely. "What is it?" She was surprised by his call. It was the middle of the afternoon, and she was in the midst of a game of cards with some of her closest friends.

"Igor is in town," Pavlov announced, equally as abrupt.

"Well, that *is* unpleasant news," she replied with disdain.

"I know that ,but we need to show the man respect, my dear."

"Don't we always?"

"Of course we do but you know…"

"Yes, of course I do but I really don't like him here in our home."

"Don't worry. I'll book a table at a restaurant, but I think you should be there." He waited for the inevitable outburst, but to his surprise, she replied gently.

"I know, just let me know where and when. Will you send Andre?"

"Sure," he replied with a sigh of relief, happy she had agreed without the usual barrage of insults she normally bestowed on him.

Chapter VII

Alicia arrived at work early the next morning, keen to finish the report on the firm's billings for the previous month. She had already finished the report by the time her boss had arrived, Stephen Hughes, who was the managing partner of Bowen & Hughes. She gave him a couple of minutes to settle before knocking on his glass door. As usual, he waved for her to enter.

"Good morning, Alicia," he said with a smile. "What can I do for you?"

"Good morning, Mr Hughes," Alicia replied. "It's just the billings for last month."

"What about them?" he asked.

"Nothing, I'm here to give you the report."

"That was quick," Stephen said as he checked the date on his rose gold IWC wristwatch. "Anything I need to know?" he asked with a solemn expression.

"No, it's all good," Alicia answered with a smile. "Invoicing is ever so slightly above budget."

She went on to ask him permission to take the rest of the day off, which was her real reason for bringing in the report. She explained she and Adrian had decided to adopt and she wanted to investigate the possibility of doing so.

"That sounds interesting! But when is the wedding? I'm assuming you'll be married before adoption since you won't stand much of a chance if you're unwed."

"Yes, we have a lot to sort out. But planning a wedding is easily done as opposed to the adoption process, which I know next to nothing about. I've heard it is a very difficult process."

"Well, knowing you like I do, Alicia, I reckon you'll soon be an authority on the subject." Stephen thought very highly of Alicia's investigative skills, which had proven to be valuable to the firm in the past.

"I hope so. Thank you, sir."

She was about to exit his office when Stephen called out to her. "Alicia, I think we know each other well enough to drop the 'sir', don't you?"

"OK, sir…" she answered without realising and added, "I think that might take time, Si…Mr Hughes." Alicia produced a hiccup of a giggle that rapidly escalated into a high-pitched squeal; the result of her futile attempt at disguising her glee. The puzzled look on Stephen's face caused a fresh bout of hysteria to gurgle up into her throat. "Right, got to go!" she nearly shouted as she quickly slipped through the door and into the corridor.

"Quite," Stephen announced to the empty room. "Women, such emotional creatures!" He shook his head as he opened the report Alicia had given him and exhaled a deep sigh, thankful that he was back on familiar ground.

When Alicia returned to her small office, she calmed herself down before calling her friend Barbara.

"Hello?" Barbara answered.

"How's the landscape looking?" Alicia said, playing on a theme that referred to their trip to Peru. "I need to tap into your resources. Are you free for lunch?"

"No can do but tomorrow I'm free...no wait, it's the other way around! So yes, I'm free. A burger at J.G. Melon would be nice. But this time, don't forget they only take cash!" Barbara was referring to the last time they had dined at J.G. Melon together. She had paid because Alicia had forgotten to bring cash.

Will she ever let that rest? Alicia thought, knowing that her friend had mentioned the incident at least twice now. "Don't you worry," she said instead. "I'll bring cash and this time, it's my treat. We better meet there as soon as we can since they don't take reservations."

"Quarter past it is," Barbara confirmed and hung up.

Alicia arrived earlier than the time she had arranged with Barbara. Since the restaurant opened at half-past eleven, she arrived at J.G. Melon's right at noon to ensure they would get a table. She ordered a Heineken and waited, watching the last few seats fill up while she fiddled with the signature green and white-checked tablecloth. Barbara was punctual as usual, and they quickly ordered two cups of chilli and two of the establishment's famous burgers. When they were settled, Alicia explained that she and Adrian were looking into the possibility of adopting and wondered if Barbara knew anyone who had experience.

"I have a cousin who adopted a little girl from...I think it was somewhere in Russia? You could speak to her; the two of you would get on *chevere*." Barbara laughed as she reached for her mobile. *Chevere* was Peruvian for 'great', or 'swell'

30

and it was a term Barbara loved using ever since returning from the trip they had taken together.

"Lucy, is that you?" Barbara asked, then paused and replied. "Yeah, just fine. And you?" She didn't wait for an answer before continuing. "I'm having lunch with a really good friend of mine. She's thinking of adopting. Would you be a darling and speak with her about it? I mean, you're an expert. Her name is Alicia." Barbara quickly handed the phone over to Alicia without giving Lucy a chance to agree or disagree.

Alicia and Lucy agreed to meet at Lucy's home after lunch. She lived on 84th street, between Lexington and Park Avenue. It was walking distance from J.G. Melon. Alicia was told to ask the doorman for Lucy Sterling. Alicia was so excited to meet Lucy that she had hardly paid any attention to what Barbara was saying during the remainder of their lunch together. As they had kissed each other goodbye, Alicia had decided it was a good thing that Barbara was self-obsessed and loved the sound of her own voice. With anyone else, Alicia would have been called out for being absent. Barbara, on the other hand, hadn't even noticed her friend's silence.

Chapter VIII

Lucy was nothing like Alicia had expected her to be. Alicia had anticipated a carbon copy of Barbara or at least someone who was entitled, vain, and bitchy. There was no denying that Barbara was very feline-like, she was sleek and beautiful, but cross her and her claws came out. She also purred when a man treated her well, both in and out of bed. Her cousin was similarly slim and well-dressed, but she was a woman who looked as if she would be more comfortable living on a ranch in Oklahoma, which was about as far removed from Barbara as possible.

Alicia had been a bit nervous at the idea of asking a stranger questions about their personal life, especially as Barbara wasn't able to accompany her. Lucy, however, was so friendly and down to earth that Alicia found it hard to believe she was Barbara's cousin and immediately felt as if they had been friends for years.

"I'm so sorry to intrude like this," Alicia apologised as she followed Lucy down the hall. "Wow, what a lovely kitchen!" She pulled out one of the tall stools from under the counter and sat upon it when Lucy motioned for her to do so.

"It is, isn't it?" Lucy giggled. "Oh Lord, I sound just like Barbara. But I just love my kitchen."

"So do I! It's gorgeous." Alicia looked around the room in awe. The kitchen, spacious with high ceilings, was modelled in a French country style. The counter and floor were made from perfectly aged solid oak with a gorgeous honey-coloured patina. The elegant cupboards, painted white, looked so authentic that Alicia would not have been surprised if they had been rescued from a crumbling French château. The whole look was pulled together with huge antique chandeliers and floor to ceiling shelves, which encompassed the entire length of one wall. Each shelf held artfully arranged items including old cookbooks, retro kitchen equipment and porcelain dinnerware.

After cutting them each a huge slice of carrot cake and pouring coffee from an old-fashioned French press, Lucy pulled a stool out from under the counter and sat next to Alicia.

"This is just *so* lovely." Alicia smiled. "Thank you so much."

"Alicia, it's fine. Besides, I get a bit bored during the day when Louisa is asleep. So, what do you want to know?" Lucy asked, returning a smile.

"Is Louisa your adopted daughter?"

"Yes, and you can meet her a bit later when she wakes up."

"That would be lovely. Well, I guess I should start at the beginning…" Alicia started explaining what had happened in her life over the last year. She spoke of her trip to Peru, meeting Adrian, being kidnapped by a cop and finally being stalked and attacked by Marion.

"Wow, you've had it rough! I remember Barbara telling me a little of what you've been through. That must have been terrible for you." Lucy spoke with genuine empathy and concern.

"Well, yes, I must say I've had better years...but now I have Adrian, and we're happy. I just think a baby will complete us." Alicia smiled a bittersweet smile. "I'm still not sure if adoption is the right way to go but I definitely want to find out more about the process."

Lucy agreed with what Alicia had said and gushed that adoption had been the perfect solution for her. She quickly explained that her extreme fibroids had caused severe scarring, and she was unable to conceive or carry a child. This was the reason why she and her husband had adopted, and they were hoping to adopt a brother or sister for Louisa in the near future. The three of them would be attending a seminar on adoption the very next day at the Hilton on 6th Avenue. "If Adrian agrees, why don't we meet up and attend the seminar together?"

"That would be fantastic," Alicia said with a huge grin. "I'll run it past Adrian later and text you either way, as long as you're sure you don't mind?"

"That'll be fine. Oh, and there's my girl!" Lucy instantly jumped up from her stool when a baby's cries began echoing through the monitor. "Come and meet her," Lucy called out as she exited the kitchen. Alicia didn't need to be asked twice and eagerly followed.

Alicia had stayed for another two hours before heading home. She was a little tired but ecstatic over the progress she had made. She couldn't wait for Adrian to return home so that she could share everything she had discovered with him. She also wanted to tell him that she had stumbled into the most beautiful experience: the sweet smell of a recently fed and freshly washed baby, nestled and content, crooning softly as she was rocked gently in cradling arms. Alicia was now hooked on the idea and knew that no matter what, she would never feel totally complete until she had a baby of her own.

Chapter IX

Alicia and Adrian were still in attendance at the adoption seminar after saying their goodbyes to Lucy and Michael Sterling. Adrian had asked them to join him and Alicia for dinner since he had liked them so much. Regrettably, the Sterlings needed to leave early to attend a prior engagement, so Lucy and Alicia agreed to talk on the phone over the next few days in order to arrange a dinner date.

Alicia, who was growing restless without the company of her new friend, had started wandering around. There was a very large crowd at the seminar, which surprised Alicia. She couldn't believe how many potential adoptive parents there were in a single room. The present speaker was very boring and droned on and on with endless statistics. Switching off, Alicia thought about the previous speaker, a man named Roland Thompson. He had caught her interest while explaining the strict rules and restrictions imposed upon adoptive parents, which was fuelling more private and so-called 'Gray adoptions' in the industry.

Alicia had made a mental note to find him and speak with him. He was currently with another couple, so Alicia and Adrian approached and waited their turn. Once the other couple began walking away, Alicia walked up to Roland and introduced herself and Adrian. "Congratulations on your speech," she added. "It was by far the most interesting."

"Thank you," Roland replied, adding in complete honesty that he was not complaining since the bureaucracy benefited people like himself. He explained that a lengthy process meant higher fees and that there was even an extra fee at the end of a successful process. He then went on to explain that he worked in both official and private adoptions and quickly produced his card. He gave it to Alicia and asked her to call him in the coming week since other prospective parents were waiting to speak with him.

Alicia and Adrian moved on and spoke with a few more agents and some other guests who, like them, were curious and eager to understand the adoption process. The crowd was thinning when Adrian claimed he was starving. He suggested it might be a good idea to go to a nearby restaurant called Patsy's. Alicia had never heard of it. "Well then, my darling," Adrian replied, "you're in for a very pleasant surprise."

Patsy's turned out to be, as Adrian had promised, a fabulous Italian restaurant. On his recommendation, they shared a bottle of Chianti Classico while dining on artichokes au gratin, which were served with lightly dressed pasta. The restaurant was stylishly decorated with the walls covered in framed autographed pictures of famous guests. Alicia fell in love with both the food and the ambience. She couldn't understand why she had never heard of the place before, especially since it wasn't far from where she had previously lived.

"So, what's your impression?" Adrian asked.

"Of the restaurant or the seminar?"

"Both," he replied with a smile.

"Well, the restaurant is absolutely wonderful. As for the seminar, I found Roland Thompson interesting." Alicia paused to take his business card out of her purse and studied it. "But not a lot else. Did you know that his agency is in Yonkers?" Alicia looked up when she asked.

"No, I didn't."

"Well, Yonkers or not, I think I should make an appointment with him. What do you think?"

Adrian agreed and they decided that Alicia would go to the appointment alone. He would accompany her to an eventual follow-up meeting. They finished their meal and took the subway back to Lincoln Center and arrived home shortly after.

"I'd love to sleep in your bed tonight," Alicia said with a playful, seductive smile as they walked into their apartment.

"You're on. I'm just going to put on my pyjamas." Adrian winked back.

"You're just *so* sexy when dressed in PJs!" Alicia teased with a giggle.

"I sure am, Babe." Adrian laughed as he grabbed her off her feet and carried her into their bedroom.

After a session of slow and gentle lovemaking, Alicia and Adrian fell asleep. Both felt very lucky to have the other. The last thing Alicia remembered before falling into a deep slumber was the touch of Adrian's lips, softly kissing her earlobe.

Chapter X

Pavlov and Yuliya were seated at the corner table in the main dining room of Très Français. They were waiting for Igor, whom their driver Andre had been sent to pick up from his hotel. Yuliya was drinking French cider and Pavlov red wine. Every now and then they would glance awkwardly at each other and then back out into the restaurant, all the while taking long gulps of their respective drinks. Neither was looking forward to dinner with the younger and vulgar, Igor.

"Why it is *so* important that I attend, I do not know," Yuliya moaned as she motioned to the waiter to bring her another drink.

"You know why, my dear," Pavlov said through clenched teeth. "Igor thinks it looks more respectable, more *normal* when a wife joins us for dinner. It draws less attention, and Igor *loves* family." He added his last remark very sarcastically.

"Yes, we both know how much he loves family," Yuliya replied in an equally sarcastic tone. They both knew that Igor had not one single shred of human kindness in any part of his body, something they had learned through bitter experience. He always insisted on being sexually entertained during his visits, and neither Pavlov nor Yuliya had lost count of the numerous girls he had disfigured and maimed. And those had been the lucky ones. There were three bodies resting in watery graves due to Igor's sadistic perversions. Pavlov was more worried than usual about Igor's peculiarities on this particular visit because the man had insisted on having Liliya's company this time, and Liliya was Pavlov's favourite. He was troubled at the thought of her safety but was, of course, unable to confide this in Yuliya.

"Here he is," Yuliya said flatly as she noticed Andre escorting Igor to their table. As the two men approached the table, Pavlov and Yuliya stood up in turns, hugging and kissing Igor on both cheeks. They acted as if they were very pleased to see him.

"How nice to see you, Igor," Yuliya said with a masterful fake smile. "What brings you all the way from Moscow this time?" she added with equally fake interest.

"Oh, just business, my dear," he replied as he kissed her cheek. "I will need to borrow your husband for just a few hours after dinner."

"But of course. Have you dined here before?" Yuliya couldn't imagine the two men speaking or their nefarious affairs in such a brightly coloured and highly frequented fine-dining establishment.

"Igor has been here before with me," Pavlov mumbled.

"Indeed, I have, and I recall having the most delicious coq au vin the last time."

"You must also try the boeuf bourguignon, it is truly delicious." Yuliya was always good at playing the gracious host.

All three of them ordered boeuf bourguignon and Pavlov asked for a bottle of Côte Roti. The dinner conversation that ensued was mostly of friends, family, and mutual acquaintances.

"So? How's your new baby?" Yuliya asked Igor. "I hear you have another fine boy." She knew Igor loved talking about his many children.

"He is strong just like his father and brothers," Igor replied with a broad smile. "It is said that I am building my own army. This may or may not be true, but all of my boys are already like me, and all will prosper."

His overbearing manner and sinister tone caused Yuliya to cringe involuntarily. To cover her faux pas, she manoeuvred herself in a way of seemingly jumping forward and raising her glass, making her wrought iron chair screech unceremoniously against the floor. "To Igor and his boys! May you all prosper in health and wealth."

"To Igor and his boys!" Pavlov had noticed his wife's disgust and desperately hoped Igor had not. He too jumped in quickly to join her in her toast.

Igor grinned and bowed his head in acknowledgement of their toast. He had seen the look of horror on Yuliya's face, as well as the subsequent reaction of Pavlov's but he had found both looks enjoyable instead of offensive. The couple had revealed they were afraid of him and his boys, and, most importantly, that they knew not to cross him or his kin. Igor loved power; he thrived on it. He also loved torture and he knew he could do so with his innuendos. A night of great food, torturous conversation, and a bit of business before the annihilation of Pavlov's favourite girl suited Igor very well. He intended to kill Liliya this time, mostly for his own pleasure but also to remind Pavlov who held all the power in their relationship. Igor grinned even wider. Oh, how he loved his life.

Chapter XI

Much to her delight, Yuliya was chauffeured home by Andre after dinner. She had stayed long enough for the sake of keeping up appearances, and Igor had wanted to discuss business with her husband. Normally she would have indulged in the restaurant's dessert menu and lingered with another order of cider, but she felt physically ill in that man's presence and was willing to forgo the crème brûlé with lavender this time.

As soon as she had exited the restaurant, Igor told Pavlov that Moscow had a new business proposal involving Ukraine. Pavlov knew better than to ask. He just nodded his head and requested the bill.

Pavlov offered Igor a cigar once they had left the restaurant. He lit one for himself as they hit the sidewalk and suggested they walk off their dinner while they waited for Andre to return. The two men strolled in the direction of the city centre for only ten minutes before Andre appeared. They wasted no time in getting into the back of Pavlov's new Mercedes, and soon they were on the motorway and heading out of town.

After half an hour or so of driving, the car slowed and took a right turn onto a small road that led them into dense woodland. Within a few minutes, they had reached a clearing and stopped in front of a large mansion. Pavlov and Igor then made their way past the ornately carved pillars that lined the entrance steps.

Instead of walking straight into the restaurant, which was blasting music and very crowded despite its remote location, the two men took a right and entered a large office adorned with antique furniture and classical artwork. Pavlov poured whiskey into two crystal tumblers before they sat down. With his glass in his hand, Igor seated himself in the crushed velvet armchair as Pavlov sat down on a vintage mahogany chair in front of him.

"So, how's business?" Igor enquired.

"Good. Very good, actually. But then, you must be fully aware of this," Pavlov said, referring to the fact that a significant percentage of his revenue had already been received in Moscow.

"Yes but I've brought with me a fresh idea to discuss with you, and it involves what is commonly referred to as 'The Magnitsky Act.' This could be very beneficial for both our countries."

"The Magnitsky Act…Does your plan have anything to do with Sergei Magnitsky?" Pavlov wasn't following Igor's train of thought.

"Sergei doesn't matter because he's dead, Pavlov. Pay attention. This will be lucrative for us both." Igor wasn't a sentimental man and never pretended to be. He spoke of death indifferently and inconsequentially.

"Lucrative? How?" Pavlov asked with genuine interest.

"Well, it has to do with Putin's response to this act. By implementing The Magnitsky Act, Obama has authorised the American government to deny entry to anyone they believe to be an offender of human rights. Putin's response? The Dima

Yakovlev Law. Essentially, the adoption of Russian children by Americans is now forbidden. Several European countries, led by the UK's government, are expected to implement similar restrictions in support of Obama's decision. Therefore, the people of these countries could face similar prohibitions on adopting from Russia. This will leave Ukraine to fill the gap. And Ukraine, like Russia, is not a signatory to the Hague Convention."

Russia had neither signed nor acceded to the convention, which held countries responsible for returning children who were internationally abducted by a parent from one participating country to another. Ukraine was one of the countries that had acceded to the convention but had not yet ratified its participation with a signature.

"Go on," Pavlov said as he leaned forward. He knew very little of The Hague Convention, and he wasn't typically interested in politics. However, he was already in the business of making money at the expense   of other human beings, and he was always interested in making more money.

"Well, Russian children could be transferred, unofficially of course, to Ukraine for adoption. They would be provided with official documentation upon arrival, which would state that they are of Ukrainian birth. This will open a new and very profitable business for us. First of all, you will need to source an orphanage in Ukraine. It needs to be one that will be able to handle babies and children coming in from Russia on top of Ukraine's own. A speedy adoption process, which will be implemented in Ukraine, will allow us to charge exorbitant fees to eager parents. The money will be collected by foreign adoption agencies, and so it will not be connected to Ukraine since it will remain offshore, in American dollars."

Pavlov was trying his best to follow. "But wouldn't this undermine the countermeasures implemented by Putin?"

"Officially, yes but this solution already has Putin's blessing, unofficially, of course. This Dima Yakovlev Law of Putin's is a direct response to Obama's attempt at barring Russian citizens from visiting or owning property in America. Obama has accused Russians of violating human rights, and Putin wants to remain strong in the face of this act. But Russia desperately needs Russian children available for adoption because there are too many of them. Russia cannot handle the situation internally, no matter what Putin says to the outside world."

"Interesting..." Pavlov replied as he took a slow puff on a fresh cigar.

"This is a new avenue for amassing a fortune," Igor continued, "a fact that is obviously not lost on Putin. Both Russians and Ukrainians will benefit from the enormous fees involved." Igor paused to watch Pavlov calculate the wealth there was to be made from the adoptions before adding, "I think it's time for me to visit the lovely Liliya, don't you?"

"Yes, yes of course." The colour instantly drained from Pavlov's face as he replied.

"I can't wait to see how her soft skin responds to my hands this time," Igor said, allowing his grin to grow even wider as he noticed the tremor of Pavlov's right hand.

"Indeed, Igor! I trust, however, that you will be kind..." Pavlov thought quickly, trying to choose his words carefully. "She is, after all, our best earner." Because she was his favourite, Pavlov had found the courage to confront his nemesis on his barbaric treatment of the girls.

"I would never hurt anyone knowingly, of course. I just don't know the extent of my own strength sometimes. You understand that don't you Pavlov?"

Pavlov nodded but he now knew that this would be Liliya's final night. As he looked at Igor's satisfied yet menacing face, he also knew that there wasn't a thing he could do about it.

Chapter XII

At eight in the morning, Alicia called Annette to tell her that she would be in later and that she had already told Stephen. This wasn't exactly the truth, however, since she was referring to yesterday's conversation with him. But she knew he would understand. Stephen gave Alicia a lot of leeway when it came to her job. This was mostly because he knew Alicia completed excellent work for the firm, but it was also partially due to the fact that he knew she'd been through some very tough times as of late. He was over-protective towards her; Alicia knew but he would never admit this to anyone.

After calling Annette, Alicia called Roland. She expressed the hope that he might be free to meet her that morning. Roland said he'd be happy to meet her in his office at eleven o'clock but that she had to make it eleven sharp since he was squeezing her in between appointments. Since she was coming from Manhattan, he advised her that the best choice would be to travel by train from Grand Central to White Plains. From there she could hail a cab to Yonkers.

At precisely ten minutes to eleven, Alicia was standing outside of Tomorrow. She pressed the intercom button and explained she had a meeting with Mr Thompson. She was buzzed in and travelled up to the third floor. The building had very little character; it was neither old nor modern and lacked any inviting qualities. However, when Alicia entered the reception area, she received a warm welcome from a friendly woman who looked to be in her early fifties. The woman's jovial manner calmed her jittery nerves.

Alicia was asked to take a seat and was offered tea, coffee or water. She requested a glass of water and accepted it gratefully after picking up one of the magazines. She had no time to read it as the receptionist returned to her side almost immediately.

"Mr Thompson is ready to see you, dear." Alicia was escorted into an empty conference room.

Roland appeared a moment later, dressed in a checked grey and blue blazer with grey slacks, black penny loafers, a striking blue tie and a plain white shirt. "Good morning, Alicia. How was your journey?" he asked politely.

"Morning! It was OK, thank you." Alicia had replied politely but she wasn't interested in small talk since they didn't have much time.

Luckily, Roland was also keen to get on with the meeting and sat down immediately. "Well, shall we go over what we briefly touched upon the other night?" He proceeded to take her through the adoption process as well as the corresponding fees. "The fee structure is pretty much standardised and will not vary much regardless of the agency you choose to work with," he explained. "I need to ask a few questions before we get started. Are you and Adrian married?"

"No, not yet but we do live together." Alicia quickly explained their living arrangements and was quietly amused when she saw a hint of surprise on Roland's face. "Is it important to be married?" she asked.

"Well, it definitely helps," Roland said. "And both of you work?"

"Yes, I am head of corporate affairs for a law firm," Alicia said as she handed him her business card, "and Adrian is a professor at NYU."

"What is your annual combined income, ballpark?" Roland asked.

"Approximately four hundred thousand."

"Will you continue working and hire a nanny?"

"Yes, that's the idea."

"So why choose to adopt when you are young enough to have children of your own?"

"Well, I'm often told that I look younger than I actually am. I will be forty in a couple of months, and I've never gone through a pregnancy. My doctor suggested that Adrian and I should, at the very least, consider the possibility of adopting instead."

"I'm going to be honest with you, Alicia. On paper, you and Adrian are not the ideal candidates. The trouble is that you're not going to make it to the top of the list because both of you are working. You must understand that nobody will be able to vet the nanny, and that's the very person who the child will end up spending most of his or her young life with, not to mention the especially crucial baby years."

"So, you think we might have a problem?" Alicia asked with a slight tremor in her voice.

"Not if you opt for private adoption."

"How is that different?"

"Well, for starters, it's expensive. It will cost you at least three times as much, perhaps more. But you will avoid all the bureaucracy since the vetting will be done essentially just by me or somebody close to me."

"What do you mean, *essentially* just by you?"

"Others will also need to sign off on the process, however, they will be relying on my opinion."

"So, is this illegal?" Alicia was shocked and had asked her question slightly louder than she had intended to.

"It's officially referred to as 'The Gray Market' if you want to do some online research; that's 'gray' spelt with an 'a' but at the end of the day, no one really cares if I'm being honest with you."

"And this is the route you would advise us to take?" Alicia had not received a solid *yes* or *no* to her previous question and was incredulous at the idea of a grey area when it came to adoption. Her tone reflected this.

"I prefer not to give my opinion. After all, it's your decision." Roland's tone, on the other hand, hadn't changed. He was calm and straightforward in his answers.

"And all the papers will be in order?" Alicia asked in a quiet voice after reflecting on his answer for a few extra seconds.

"Yes, they will."

"And the baby, will it be local or foreign?"

"It could be either."

"If we choose to adopt an infant from another country, how will that work?"

"The biological parents will be foreign, of course, but the baby will become a US citizen as part of the adoption process since both adoptive parents will have US citizenship. You and your partner will have both been processed and cleared for foreign adoption."

"Is there any chance that the biological parents could later claim the baby?"

"As opposed to a domestic adoption, this could never happen if the child is foreign because he or she would become a US citizen as soon as they have been adopted."

Roland had answered with a smile in an attempt to ease the tension in the room but Alicia didn't return his smile. "And this is guaranteed?" she asked.

"It is," Roland responded without missing a beat.

"Which countries are we talking about?"

"Many different countries, although I personally work almost exclusively with babies from Ukraine."

"Why Ukraine?"

Roland remained stiff and business-like. His answers provided essential information yet they seemed limited and without many details. "Russia no longer allows US citizens to adopt infants from their country, thus making Ukraine an increasingly attractive alternative."

Something about 'increasingly attractive alternative' had rubbed Alicia the wrong way. She didn't like the phase Roland had chosen, and she didn't like the way he had said it. "So, are they all white and presumably blonde?" She had asked the question with her anger building audibly.

Roland continued in his usual fashion, without pause and undeterred from what Alicia had said. "I cannot comment on that, but you will of course be able to view photographs."

"But this sounds like trading in humans instead of adoption to me."

"I will disregard your comment, Alicia. We are talking about babies whose biological parents are either unable or unwilling to raise their children. By arranging these adoptions, we're ensuring that these children have a decent life filled with love and proper care instead of living a life of extreme poverty, abuse, or worse. I would hardly say that this is trading in humans, and if it is, it is done for all the right reasons." Roland's voice was polite but clipped.

"I didn't mean to be offensive, Mr Thompson." Alicia was being sincere, realising she had harshly judged Roland instead of the system. "Please forgive me."

"These matters are often quite complex. My advice to you is that you should always proceed in accordance with your own conscience if you want to go through with an adoption. Only work with an agent you feel comfortable with. I am only outlining the landscape as it exists, Alicia. I am not the architect of this plan. I am simply trying to place as many children as possible into the hands of people who can offer them a brighter future." He paused to look at his watch. "Perhaps we should stop here. Take some time to absorb what I have told you and discuss everything I've shared with you with Adrian. I also think that you might want to consider contacting other agencies in order to learn more. Does this sound reasonable to you?"

"Yes, thank you," Alicia spoke as she stood up. "I will do that and then perhaps arrange a follow-up meeting with you?"

"That would be my pleasure." Roland smiled as he outstretched his hand, but his smile didn't reach his eyes as the last one had. Alicia realised that he might still be slightly annoyed with what she had said.

"Thank you," Alicia said again, making a point of returning his smile.

Alicia made it back to Manhattan just after lunch, having consumed only half of a turkey wrap and a few sips of coke on the train. Both had looked appealing to her when she had made the purchase, but she had been unable to stomach either of them. She left work shortly after arriving because she had been unable to concentrate.

Once home, she poured herself a neat whiskey, had a shower, and put on her pyjamas. She then poured herself a second whiskey to replace the one she had already gulped down and opened a bag of Cheetos, her favourite comfort food. She had called Adrian before her shower and told him they had a lot to discuss when he got home. He had promised not to be late.

Lying on the couch, savouring her Cheetos and whiskey, Alicia decided that a Chinese takeaway or a pizza would do for dinner now that her appetite had returned to her. *I'll let Adrian decide between the two*, she thought as she closed her eyes in an attempt to ease the pain in her temples. Within a few minutes her breathing had slowed, and she was able to fall asleep. She would soon recount her dream to Adrian, of babies stacked upon babies, housed in cattle pens with auction numbers stuck to their backs. She would sob in despair when he woke her up, beseeching him, "We must adopt, Adrian. Oh, please say we can adopt…"

Chapter XIII

At the same time as Alicia was dreaming of babies being auctioned off like cattle, Pavlov, who now had ties with several orphanages, was overseeing examinations. A doctor, whom the current orphanage had hired, was assessing baby after baby. At twenty-five thousand American dollars each, Pavlov estimated that the current baby crop was worth just under the sum of three million dollars. *How fast can the money be collected?* he asked himself as he watched the doctor listening to a baby boy's heartbeat with a stethoscope. But Pavlov hardly noticed the babies or at least he tried not to. To him, they were money, pure and simple. Therefore, without too much to distract him, he answered his own question and estimated that the cash would take about two months tops to roll in.

The idea was to find nice (and wealthy) adoptive parents in America, Canada, Australia, or Italy. However, this wasn't for Pavlov's love of humanity but because he knew that people would do anything to gain their heart's desire, especially if that desire happened to belong to a woman who was yearning for a baby. He also knew that if suitable candidates were not forthcoming from these countries, there was always the option of selling the babies to buyers in Thailand or Indonesia, countries that were rife with child prostitution. But even Pavlov – who had built an empire on

54

prostitution – was very uncertain of this option. The idea had been Igor's, and although Pavlov had agreed, he didn't like the sound of it. He just hoped that he knew people as well as he thought he did and that there were hundreds of childless couples out there, desperate for a baby from Ukraine. He was disgusted with the thought of the alternative, which meant that he would be selling children into a destitute and dangerous life of continuous abuse. Even for a man like himself, the thought of child prostitution was repulsive and something he wasn't so certain he could facilitate or even contribute to.

Chapter XIV

Alicia awoke restless and slightly irritated. After hours of talking to Adrian about Ukrainian babies, she had ended up sobbing in his arms and falling asleep before even hearing his opinion on the matter. Therefore, when the still emotionally bruised Alicia awoke to find Adrian wasn't beside her, she wasn't at all pleased. Her irritation wasn't abated when she found a note sticking out from under the coffee pot:

My Darling,
I needed to leave early, and I didn't want to wake you.
Call me later.
Love you,
Adrian xxx

She picked up the house phone from the kitchen counter and punched in Adrian's office number, the call went straight to voicemail. Alicia hung up and slammed the phone back down. After drinking a coffee, she felt a little less stressed and once again picked up the phone but this time she called Barbara.

Once Barbara answered, Alicia began by thanking her friend for introducing her to Lucy. Alicia described Barbara's cousin as a total darling. She then went on to tell Barbara all about yesterday's meeting with Roland Thompson. To her disappointment, Barbara was far from sympathetic. "Calm down," she responded plainly. "You want a baby, and a baby would certainly be happy with you and Adrian as parents. So, what's the big deal? What better alternatives are out there?"

"Yeah, I know all that but it's the ethical side that worries me!" Alicia exclaimed.

"Forget ethics, Alicia! All you need to know about ethics is that you will be giving a child a chance at a better life. You just need to make sure that the documentation is in perfect order, which shouldn't be too difficult for you. You work for a frigging law firm if I'm not mistaken."

"But my firm works with litigation and arbitration, not with birth certificates and adoptions!" Alicia protested weakly.

"Sure but you must have access to certain resources?" Barbara asked the question rhetorically and continued before Alicia could answer. "So, get off your moral high horse and start thinking!"

She's right, Alicia thought to herself. *Who am I to question everything and everybody?* But to Barbara, she said, "I am going to visit other agencies to verify what Roland said."

"Now that sounds perfectly reasonable," Barbara responded. Alicia could hear the smile in her friend's voice. However, the thought of her friend smiling evaporated when Barbara screamed, "Gosh! I must rush! But call me tomorrow because I want to know what Adrian says about all of this." Alicia agreed to call Barbara the next day. Then they said their goodbyes and hung up.

Twenty minutes later, a freshly showered and neatly dressed Alicia headed out onto the sidewalk while answering her ringing mobile. "Hello?" she answered and placed the phone between her ear and shoulder.

"Hello, Darling. I just wanted to apologise for leaving this morning." Adrian's smooth, masculine voice echoed down the phone.

"It's fine," Alicia said, bypassing the fact that his early morning departure had annoyed her. Instead of bringing it up, Alicia went through some of the adoption details again while she walked. She also shared her doubts and her earlier phone conversation with Barbara. Adrian explained that he understood her concerns and feelings following the meeting with Roland. He also said that, while it was typical of Barbara to set aside any moral concerns, she was probably right in her comments about having everything examined by an experienced lawyer. Providing everything stood up to the test, there was no need to worry so much. Adrian suggested they investigate the possibility of having his sperm implanted in a womb for hire and Alicia immediately rejected this idea. She openly admitted that she would be jealous of the fact that he would be related to their baby, and she wouldn't. Adrian could see where she was coming from and let his suggestion go.

They cut their conversation short because Adrian had a lecture to conduct. After a couple of hours, Adrian called Alicia back. After further discussing adoption versus pregnancy, they decided to continue exploring both avenues. The first step would be to make an appointment with a fertility specialist. It was possible that a specialist-assisted pregnancy might mitigate some of the risks involved for Alicia. Secondly, they agreed to find out more information from other adoption agencies.

"We could take a couple of days off work to investigate our options, I mean, given the importance of all this," Adrian suggested. Alicia warmed to his thinking since he seemed to want a family just as much as she did. She felt a sudden throbbing rush of love for Adrian. She knew that, whatever happened, they would work things out and get their baby, of this, she had no doubt.

Chapter XV

Alicia had called Elisabeth the night before, explaining that she and Adrian needed to see a specialist. She hadn't thought about the conversation since and had only informed her friend because she had requested to be kept in the loop on their baby plans. So, without expecting to hear anything from Elisabeth over the next couple of days, Alicia was quite surprised to get a call from her that following morning, informing Alicia that she had managed to secure an appointment for her with a specialist. Alicia immediately called Adrian back and left a voice message to say they were booked in to see an expert that very afternoon at half-past five. She stated that the doctor they were seeing had come highly recommended through Elisabeth's extensive network.

By the time Adrian had arrived at the address Alicia had given him, Alicia had already gone in for an examination. Adrian was asked to wait while Dr Douglas Madison examined her. A little later, he joined Alicia in Dr Madison's office. The doctor said that Alicia was in good health but stated the risks involved, which they were already familiar with. The doctor explained that if they chose to go ahead with the pregnancy under his watch, he would select two high-quality sperm from a sample provided by Adrian. He would have both implanted in Alicia and they would subsequently monitor the pregnancy very carefully to try to minimise the risks involved. He asked if Alicia would prefer to have a caesarean section or a normal delivery, and Alicia said she'd prefer the latter. He listed the risks involved before briefly covering the other risks should she need to have a caesarean. They agreed on two things: the termination of the pregnancy if the foetus was not developing normally, and a caesarean if Alicia's pregnancy extended beyond her expected due date. "All of this is to protect both the mother and the child," Dr Madison explained. "Furthermore, you should also know that implanting two sperm means that the chance of twins is a distinct possibility." He stressed that all pregnancies involved risks but giving birth at Alicia's age, even as a first full-term pregnancy, wasn't as uncommon as some people might think. The statistics were actually on her side.

Upon leaving Dr Madison's practice, both Alicia and Adrian were feeling upbeat and walking casually, touching each other's fingers every now and again. Suddenly, Alicia impulsively reached for her phone and dialled Eric Holstein's number. Eric picked up immediately and she was pleased to hear her friend's voice booming through her mobile.

"You shall never die, Ms Byrne."

"What on earth are you talking about, Eric?" Alicia giggled while she spoke.

"An old expression," Eric said with a chuckle. "When somebody you're thinking about calls you, they supposedly become immortal," he said.

"Well, that is good news, I guess but I was really calling you on the off-chance that you were free to have dinner with Adrian and me."

"I could do dinner, sure. What about Rotisserie Georgette on 60th between Madison and Fifth?"

"Sounds great. What time?" Alicia asked.

"How about seven-thirty? I'll book a table for four since I will be bringing someone."

"Perfect! See you then." Alicia ended the call.

"So," Adrian said, "are you going to fill me in?"

"Oh, Darling, we are hunting for opinions, remember? And you will not believe this; Eric said he's bringing someone." Alicia said it as she moved her eyebrows up and down in a suggestive but comical way.

"OK, where are we going?" Adrian asked, grinning uncontrollably.

"Rotisserie Georgette on 60th, between Madison and Park."

"That's great, I haven't been there for ages." Alicia marvelled at the thought of how the promise of good food won Adrian over every time.

"When were you last there?" Alicia asked but then continued before he could answer, "I've never been, so naturally, I'm wondering who you've been there with." Alicia composed herself and sported a serious expression.

"Oh, come off it. We both had lives before we met, not nearly as fulfilling but…" He trailed off, dreading an argument.

"Darling, I'm kidding!" But Alicia heard Adrian's sigh of relief and the realisation that she had been very insecure of late hit her. She knew her insecurities bothered him a lot more than he let on. Alicia made a mental note to try controlling her paranoia – and her jokes about it – so that it never came between her and Adrian.

Since they had some time to kill before dinner, Adrian suggested they go to the restaurant early. "They have a great bar, so let's have a drink there rather than trudging around, trying to find somewhere else," he said.

Upon entering the simple but very elegant restaurant, Alicia exclaimed, "What a charming place!" Some parts of the walls were tiled, whereas others sported antique mirrors held in brass frames of different designs and sizes. The spit-roasted game was on display for the patrons to see and the smell of the place was divine. But Alicia was hardly surprised because Eric Holstein's taste, be it in restaurants, bars, or anything else, was exquisite.

Eric turned up twenty-five minutes later, accompanied by a younger man. They were seated and Eric poured the bottle of Bordeaux he had ordered upon arrival while he introduced his guest. "This is my nephew, Sebastian." Once the glasses were poured, each guest picked one up and toasted the occasion.

"Here, anything and everything roasted is delicious," Eric said.

"Amen to that!" Adrian replied, making the first-timers Alicia and Sebastian smile in anticipation.

They ordered their food and another bottle of wine. Alicia loved her rustic dish of roast chicken with roasted potatoes.

"So, Alicia. What can I do for you?" Eric asked.

"I didn't say I needed…" Alicia tried protesting before Eric interrupted her.

"You didn't call me at six-forty on a whim to see if I was free for dinner."

"And why not?" Alicia said defensively.

"Because that isn't like you. You forget that I know you pretty well by now, and I am all ears."

"Well," she said as she turned to Adrian, "darling, why don't you help me out here?"

Adrian explained in a very simple and composed way that they wanted to have children and had debated on whether to conceive or opt for adoption. He explained Alicia's concerns regarding both private and official adoptions before explaining the risks of pregnancy at her age.

"And we have just seen a doctor by the name of Douglas Madison, who's a specialist of pregnancy in mature women," Alicia added but she didn't want to elaborate on the appointment. Instead, she reinforced her concerns about the legality of private adoptions since they could involve babies of uncertain origins and nationalities.

Eric nodded and explained that this was an area he was eager to research. "It could well be broaching the area of human smuggling," he said. "I've heard stories of abandoned or stolen children who had been sold into different types of slave trading or sexual abuse. There are also reports of women confessing they had been paid to give birth to babies who were otherwise destined for abortion." Eric was of the opinion that every child adopted was a child saved from slavery, abuse, or being slaughtered for their organs. "Hard to comprehend it all, really, since a single organ is worth more on the black market than a whole living baby up for adoption. The question is more about sourcing," he finished sadly.

Eric's point about sourcing was key since Alicia herself couldn't believe the people dealing in human organ harvesting could be the same people who worked on providing babies for international adoptions. What if the sourcing coincided? *And paedophiles*, she wondered. *Where do they find babies and small children to make their sick films? What if offering babies up for adoption is a mere by-product of something much larger and much more sinister?* These thoughts made Alicia shiver.

Alicia was disgusted and outraged at the thought of what desperate people did for money. Alicia had secretly come to the same conclusion as Eric and was feeling happier from this afternoon's meeting than yesterday's. The problem was that whatever she decided to do wouldn't have any impact whatsoever in a broader sense. She decided there and then that she was going to investigate the subject of private adoption, irrespective of her and Adrian's decision to adopt or not.

Chapter XVI

The next morning at ten o'clock, Alicia was waiting in an adoption agency to see Mrs Sarah Cohen. The agency was located in mid-town, and the décor inside the agency was typically old-fashioned, showing no signs of a recent upgrade. She was told that Mrs Cohen was running late but should be in shortly. Indeed, just fifteen minutes later, Alicia and Mrs Cohen were shaking hands and exchanging greetings. Alicia was then escorted into a meeting room by Mrs Cohen herself.

Sarah Cohen was a tall and slender woman in her early fifties. She sat down at the head of a rectangular table after seating Alicia on her right-hand side. She then placed a business card in front of Alicia, who followed suit.

"You're a lawyer?"

"No, I'm just a paralegal," Alicia replied with a smile.

"Well, hardly *just* a paralegal if you're head of corporate affairs. You're interested in adopting a child, I presume?"

No, I am here to help you redecorate your offices, Alicia thought to herself sarcastically. "Yes, we're looking into the possibility of adopting."

"And 'we' means you and your husband, yes?"

"We're not married yet but we live together." Alicia could see just a hint of disappointment in Sarah's eyes.

"And your husband, sorry, your boyfriend. What does he do?"

"He is a professor of economics at NYU," Alicia said proudly.

"So financially you're doing fine, even though you will probably need to hire a nanny if you both continue working?"

"That's correct. Is that a problem?" Alicia asked, already knowing the answer.

"In an official adoption, which cynically can be viewed as a beauty contest, you would not figure amongst the strongest contenders. Do you have children of your own? And can I call you Alicia?"

"Yes, of course, please call me Alicia. And no, I don't have children of my own."

"Why, may I ask?" Sarah asked as she looked up from the table.

"It is only now that I find myself in a relationship where both of us want children. I'm going to be forty in a couple of months. I was pregnant a few months ago but I was stabbed and lost the baby. The hospital staff who cared for me said that I might have trouble carrying a child again. This combined with the risks involved with a pregnancy at my age…Well, let's just say that it makes adoption a very strong contender."

"Yes, I understand where you're coming from. You might want to consider a private adoption, in which case, I can refer you to someone."

"So, you don't handle private adoptions yourself?"

"No, I'm afraid I don't."

"May I ask why? I have been led to believe that they are similar."

"Well, I don't know who you've been talking to, but private adoptions are most commonly sought out by people

67

who wish to avoid all the red tape involved with official adoption. As I've already partially explained, official adoptions can be a very difficult process, and you'll probably only be considered if you're married, wealthy, and a stay-at-home mum. There are also the criminal background checks, the psychiatric tests, and the list of boxes you need to tick off can seem endless. There aren't many people who pass every test, and so that's why a lot of people, especially if they're wealthy enough, will choose to go down the private route."

"Could you please enlighten me a bit more?" Alicia asked as she leaned forward in her chair.

"Well, an official adoption is when the biological parents give up their child to the official authorities for adoption. The authorities then rely upon people like me to find the most suitable adoptive home. As I have just said, this involves a lot of red tape and bureaucracy. In a private adoption, the authorities have little or no involvement, which is normally to do with the biological parents' wishes. In most cases, there are no conditions. However, when arranged through an adoption agency like mine, everything still needs to be done by the book. This is because we're supervised by the authorities, and they've implemented very high standards. The authorities are not just worried about people breaking the law but about the welfare of the child. The child's wellbeing is paramount, which brings us back to the red tape…"

"So, what you're saying is that adoption agencies like yours are seldom involved with private adoptions because it only complicates an otherwise fairly straightforward process?"

"You could say that, although I would probably describe it slightly differently," Sarah said with a small, crooked smile.

"But you have no problem referring me to somebody working in private adoptions?"

"No, I have a reciprocal arrangement with an agency that specialises in private adoptions."

"Can you give me their name, please?" Alicia asked even though she already had a feeling where this was going.

"Of course, it's a small agency out in Yonkers. It's called Tomorrow Adoption Agency."

"So, they only handle private adoptions?" Alicia asked. Albeit Roland had told her that they handle official adoptions as well as private ones.

"They do but not just national adoptions. If I'm not mistaken, they also specialise in international adoptions."

"Well, this has been a very informative meeting. Is it alright if I call you Sarah?" Alicia asked.

"Of course, it is, and good luck to you. Please take this booklet with you. It describes the various phases and the fees involved. The fee for each phase is pretty much standard and doesn't really vary from one agency to another."

"Thank you, and thanks again for seeing me at such short notice. You've been very helpful," Alicia said as she stood and shook Sarah's hand.

"You're welcome. Glad to be of service and best of luck again with whatever you decide." Sarah's crooked smile was up again and still genuine.

Alicia left the agency and walked briskly to work. It was a beautiful sunny day, and the offices of Bowen & Hughes were less than eight blocks away. Taking her phone out of her purse, she noticed that she had missed two calls, one from Barbara and another from Eric. She was more intrigued by the call from Eric since she had only seen him the night before, so she decided to return his call first. She also already knew what Barbara was calling about.

"Hi, Eric. What's up?" Alicia quickly added how much she had enjoyed their meal and his company, as well as his nephew's, the night before.

Eric jumped straight to the point. "Can you do lunch in, say, an hour? Let's do something light, perhaps Le Colonial? I have something I'd like to run by you."

"Sure," Alicia replied, recalling how Eric has always gone out of his way to help her. He had done it recently with a case of hers that had involved fraud, which had ultimately led to her promotion at work.

After saying goodbye and hanging up, Alicia tried calling Barbara. The call went straight to voicemail.

Chapter XVII

Eric was already seated at their usual table when Alicia arrived. She looked at her watch, concerned, as Eric rose from his seat while shaking his head. After kissing her on the cheek, he said, "You're not late. I was early, so I ordered our usual. I hope that's OK with you?"

"Of course, that's fine," Alicia replied, returning his kiss.

Eric continued before Alicia had the chance to settle in. "There are actually two items I want to run by you. The first is that I have received a proposal from Peru to now set up the English equivalent of the Behaviour Society."

The Behaviour Society or 'comportamientosociedad.com' (which is Spanish for Behaviour Society) was how Alicia and Eric first met when he was looking for participants for the eventual English version to share their thoughts online on how the world could be improved and become a better place.

"The idea is that the two websites will communicate with each other. I personally know the woman who is in charge of administering both the website and the blog in Spanish, and she is very good at what she does. The opportunity seems to be legitimate and intriguing. What do you think?"

"I think it sounds very exciting! First of all, Spanish is widely spoken throughout the world. Having the site in Spanish is important and having a sister site in English will be advantageous. Secondly, I think that having a website that's already been established and was successful enough to create another one in English means it'll be successful. And it will probably, hopefully, go smoothly, thanks to the lessons learnt from launching the dry run Spanish website."

Eric was nodding eagerly while Alicia spoke. "My thoughts precisely. So that's what we'll do then. How's your Spanish, Alicia?"

"Not great, I'm afraid. My Spanish is limited to my one trip to Peru, and the majority of the time I ended up speaking English to other tourists like myself."

"Oh well, we'll leave that be then. Now, onto the second topic of official versus private adoptions. Can you see yourself working with me on this?"

"Absolutely!" Alicia brightened. "I have already started researching the subject myself and I have actually just come from a very interesting meeting with an adoption agency, where we discussed at length the pros and cons of both private and official adoption."

"Ah! You never disappoint, Alicia. I had a feeling you would already be checking out various agencies and how they operate. So, we have a deal, then?" Eric outstretched his hand.

"Deal!" Alicia replied, shaking his hand enthusiastically.

They proceeded to devour a variety of small Vietnamese dishes that were placed on their table at regular intervals. Alicia was happy to be with Eric in the warm lighting, surrounded by the eclectic variety of framed black and white photographs and indoor palm plants. They dropped their formal business tone of conversing and engaged in the kind of small talk characteristic of very close friends.

Alicia worked hard once she returned to the office that afternoon. Her work had been piling up due to her absences over the last few days. Barbara called back, and although Alicia answered, she didn't have the time to talk. She suggested meeting up after work rather than speaking over the phone. Barbara agreed to come to Alicia's neck of the woods. They made plans for half-past six at the Metro Roof Bar. Alicia arrived precisely at the designated time. Barbara was already there and had managed to snag one of the last tables.

"Well, hello there!" Alicia smiled at her friend.

"Hi," Barbara said quickly while returning her smile. "Have you got some lubricant? Let me see what's in your bag." She was joking but only started laughing when Alicia started blushing. Barbara was referring to an intimate conversation the pair had had about anal sex a few months before.

"Oh, for God's sake, Barbara! Don't be so rude. Can't you see that I'm embarrassed?" Alicia exclaimed.

Alicia's outburst only caused Barbara to laugh harder. When she had calmed down slightly, she said, "They say it's like your AMEX card – 'Don't leave home without it!'" This caused her to burst out into hysterical laughter all over again.

"How dare you!" Alicia said in mock anger, but she had also started laughing even though Barbara had used this joke before. Alicia was too kind to point this out. *This one is hopeless,* she thought to herself but silently cursed herself for letting Barbara in on one of her most intimate concerns. However, it was a lesson learned and not something Alicia would repeat.

"So, tell me about your upcoming adoption. What did Adrian say? And have you visited any other adoption agencies?" Barbara asked.

"I visited a Jewish adoption agent today who said that she only worked with official adoptions. The most interesting part was that she told me the agency I visited before *only* partakes in private adoptions. She said that she refers clients to Roland and vice versa."

"Doesn't that give you more confidence, then?" Barbara asked, suddenly serious.

"I'm not sure what you mean," Alicia answered.

"Well, it seems to add up. I mean, each agency having its own special focus makes sense in any competitive industry. Plus, if this woman is referring you to them, she must think they act ethically and above board. I would assume she works to stringent rules and regulations if she only deals in *official* adoptions."

"Well, they certainly don't seem to compete much on price," Alicia said, adding that prices for an official adoption were almost the same save for the hint of a huge payout somewhere along the way with a private adoption. "One reads almost like a carbon copy of the other in theory, apart from the fact that a private adoption means most of the boxes will be ticked off instantly, with virtually no background checks at all," Alicia added that she thought there should be some checks along the way considering the safety of children's lives were at stake.

"You're too suspicious about everything," Barbara said with a simple shrug of her shoulders before looking up at the waitress, who had just appeared with their drinks.

Alicia was grateful for the interruption since she felt the need to recompose herself before proceeding with the conversation. Barbara, as always, seemed to have the upper hand in their exchange of words. "Yesterday, Adrian and I went to see a doctor who specialises in assisted pregnancies for mature women. Both of us came away very optimistic, so I haven't ruled out giving birth myself just yet."

"Gosh, it all sounds a bit confusing to me!" Barbara exclaimed.

"No, not really...It's such an important decision. Evaluating all our options surely makes sense?" Alicia was slightly irritated and hoped her tone hadn't given her away.

"Well, I usually just go ahead with things based on my instinct." As in all things, it was Barbara's way or the highway.

"Yes, well, I've noticed that, but I tick a little differently..."

"You don't say...Like chalk and cheese, us two!"

They ordered more drinks and the conversation turned into small talk, enabling Alicia to ponder how different they were from each other. *The one thing we have in common*, Alicia reflected, *is that we somehow seem to enjoy each other's company.* However, she decided that after today's encounter, Barbara needed to be digested in smaller and less frequent portions.

Chapter XVIII

Alicia and Adrian were on the train travelling to White Plains, and from there they would catch a cab to Yonkers. Roland Thompson had agreed to see them at nine-thirty that morning. When they arrived, Betsy showed them inside the meeting room in her usual friendly way. Surprisingly, Roland was with them almost instantly. They then exchanged the usual pleasantries before sitting down. Roland and Alicia both placed notepads in front of themselves. But as soon as Roland had sat down, he stood up again and asked, "Can I offer anyone something to drink?"

Adrian asked for a glass of water, whereas Alicia and Roland opted for coffee. *He takes his black without sugar or sweetener just as I do*, Alicia noticed. She then questioned herself for studying Roland so intently. Studying people had become a habit of Alicia's. It all started when she had been kidnapped by a cop who was meant to be protecting her. Taking sharp observations of even the tiniest actions made by others was of course due to her ordeal and the subsequent injuries she had received during the kidnap. Her suspicion and distrust of anyone new might have eased off if she hadn't been stalked and finally stabbed by Marion a few months later. But these events did happen back-to-back, and the result was that Alicia was paranoid and nervous at times, especially around strangers. She had become quite an intense observer of people, and although she did this in the hope of gaining insight into the character and personality of whomever she was studying, she also knew that it made some people uncomfortable. But she couldn't stop herself, no matter how hard she tried to.

"So, let's recap, shall we?" Roland said, backtracking a bit more than necessary because he loved to put on a bit of show for his clients. "We first met at the conference at the Hilton, correct?" He continued before either of them could answer his question. "You and I had a lengthy meeting the following week," he said while nodding his head in Alicia's direction, "during which you demonstrated some concerns regarding private adoption. You said you would like to talk things over with Adrian, and here we are again." He finished his small speech without any eye contact as if he had just been talking to the room instead of Alicia and Adrian.

Alicia wanted to ask if they could just get on with it, but she stopped herself. "You also advised me to contact other agents for comparison, which I have done." Roland and Adrian both nodded in agreement, so Alicia continued. "So, we are here to talk about private adoption, which I've now discovered is the type of adoption you specialise in."

"We tend to conduct more private than official adoptions here, yes. Is that what you're getting at, Alicia?"

"That's precisely what I'm getting at. In fact, your name came up in a meeting with another agent, who shall remain nameless. I was told that she refers all business of private adoptions to you," Alicia stated.

"Ah, so you've been speaking to Sarah Cohen, who works exclusively with official adoptions. I trust that she also made it clear that we refer business to her, and that there is no financial arrangement between us whatsoever," Roland explained.

"Yes, she did mention that. She also mentioned that your expertise seems to principally cover overseas adoptions. Is that right?"

"We do both," he said. "But private adoptions are less risky when they take place overseas."

"Less risky? Why is that?" Alicia asked.

"It has to do with anonymity," Roland replied.

"*Anonymity?*" Alicia repeated, both shocked and confused.

"Let me give you the rundown on how it works, and you'll understand," Roland said slickly with his charming smile back in place. "First of all, in domestic private adoption, you can come across pregnant women who'll demand down payments from multiple potential adoptive parents, purely for financial gain. Quite often, these women have no intention whatsoever of giving up their child for adoption. National private adoption normally means the physical transfer of the child upon birth. The biological parents and the adoptive parents will have become acquainted at some point, either during the pregnancy or after the birth, and will have agreed upon the terms. However, it can happen that the biological parents, usually the mothers, can later regret giving up a child and decide to take legal action, usually with success, to have their child returned to them. I've also come across cases where potential adoptive parents finance an entire pregnancy only to find out that the biological mother doesn't want to give up her child and so the adoption never takes place. I could go on and on."

"And this doesn't happen overseas?" Alicia asked.

"No, it doesn't," Roland replied.

"And why is that?"

"Well, for one thing, there will never be a physical transfer between the biological and adoptive parents. An authorised intermediary does the transfer. A perfect example of this is Ukraine's own adoption process, which is handled by the state through an authority known as the SDAPRC. Adoption agencies, as we know them here, do not exist as a principle of law in Ukraine. However, in practice, the ultimate decision lies with a judge who resides in the region where the child is born."

"What about marriage? Is that a requirement?" Adrian sat forward while speaking out for the first time, looking at Roland.

"In Ukraine, it is a requirement. However, as you probably know, all you need is a valid driving license to get married here. And, in places like the state of Virginia, the marriage certificate can be obtained on the very same day."

"It sounds pretty straightforward to me," Adrian said as he sat back in his chair.

"Well, that's because it is!" Roland exclaimed with a grin.

"OK, so what are the costs associated with private adoption?" Adrian asked his question in a very straightforward manner and without a smile.

"A little over thirty thousand, plus your travel expenses. Except, in Ukraine, the cost could easily be double that."

"And why is that?" It was now Adrian instead of Alicia who was asking all the questions.

"Well, this is due to the bureaucracy or, rather, the lack thereof. If you're willing to pay a little extra, then it is by far the fastest, cleanest, and most watertight method of adoption that you will come across. It usually takes at least twelve months in other countries but in Ukraine, it can take as little as a couple of months."

"And how is that payable?" Adrian asked.

"You pay forty percent up-front and sixty percent upon completion," Roland answered.

"Is the forty percent refundable if the adoption doesn't go through?" Alicia asked.

"If you decide not to go through with the adoption, the expenses incurred are not refundable. Other items, like the eventual deposits in escrow, will be partially returned."

They said goodbye to Roland and Alicia was back in her Manhattan office just over an hour later. She quickly called Eric and told him about her meeting with Roland.

"I am still leaning toward the idea of pregnancy but if you decide your new website could foot the bill, I'd be willing to go through with the process of a private adoption with Mr Thompson. Alternatively, I could write you a detailed report on the information I have thus far, which should be enough to stir up some excitement among the website's investors."

Eric said he needed some time to come up with a plan of action and promised to call Alicia back as soon as he could.

Chapter XIX

Donetsk is the capital of Donbas, a region in eastern Ukraine and southwestern Russia. The industrial city is reportedly home to over two million inhabitants. It is the fifth-largest city in Ukraine, but the people of this region mostly speak Russian. Due to its self-proclaimed independence, Donetsk is no longer under the effective control of Ukrainian authorities. The proletarian, left-wing uprising in the region is aimed at independence from both the central government in Kyiv and the influence of Moscow. Therefore, the bitterness of the region's working class is very much aimed at local businesses, as well as the middle class. The region has become a mostly lawless society, riddled with military conflict, and spurned by both the east and the west.

It is mostly prohibited for foreigners to enter Donetsk from Ukraine. Teaching the Ukrainian language has been almost entirely abolished and armed conflict has been ongoing for several years. The orphanages of Donbas were in a particularly bad state, so it was no surprise when the local authorities welcomed Pavlov Andreiko's offer of financial aid. The fact that he could also unofficially assist with international adoptions of the orphaned infants of the region was of particular interest to the judge, who had the authority to grant all necessary permits. His name was Vladimir Kovalenko and he had personally warmed to the proposed involvement of Pavlov, so much so that he made sure the necessary paperwork was arranged immediately with nearly zero questions asked. It wasn't difficult for him to realise this deal would provide some much-needed financial aid for the orphans, the community in general, and of course, himself. The fact that many of the orphans were born on the wrong side of the Ukrainian border made no difference to him whatsoever.

Chapter XX

Alicia and Adrian were busy making dinner together, which meant Adrian was cooking and Alicia was pouring wine. This routine was one they shared most evenings, and Alicia would set the table and do the dishes, whilst Adrian prepared their meal. Tonight, Adrian was making his famous spaghetti carbonara, which Alicia absolutely loved. Adrian had purchased Italian pancetta instead of American bacon, and he had diced the pancetta into small cubes tossing it in a sizzling pan until it was perfectly golden in colour. In another pan, there was half a cup of finely diced onion, which he had gently fried over a low heat so that the slices turned opaque and didn't brown. The final ingredients, which were lined up and ready on the kitchen counter were one cup of Parmesan and one cup of cream. Alicia, who had finished her chores, sat at the table sipping her wine as she watched Arian expertly drain and rinse the spaghetti once it was perfectly al dente. He then added the other ingredients and stirred them into the steaming pasta, which was finally served in large white bowls and garnished with Parmesan shavings. The strong Chianti Alicia had already poured accompanied the dish.

When they first started eating, they didn't talk much since they were both hungry and too intent on devouring the meal. However, after a few minutes, Alicia started to feel full and suggested they have a conversation about their options. "So, what's your conclusion so far on the baby issue? Pregnancy or adoption?" she asked as she forked another huge mound of spaghetti into her mouth.

Adrian took a sip of his wine and said, "I'm happy with whatever you decide. Please don't focus on the financial aspect, as that doesn't even come into the equation. A specialist-monitored pregnancy is probably just as expensive as a private adoption. The truth is, Alicia, it's your body, and I hope you know that you can count on my full support no matter what you decide to do."

"Thank you for saying that Baby," Alicia gushed as she reached out and took his hand. "But I might end up doing both…" She went on to explain her earlier conversation with Eric and their mutual interest in investigating the issues surrounding private adoption, particularly private overseas adoption. Adrian wasn't shocked by Alicia's news and reiterated his support for whatever she decided to do.

Chapter XXI

Alicia called Eric the following day. After a few words spent exchanging pleasantries, they agreed to a brainstorming session later that afternoon. They met at the Regency Bar on Park Avenue. Alicia immediately began their meeting by repeating everything she had told him on the phone about adopting from Ukraine but this time in greater detail.

Eric listened attentively. "Let me see if I understand correctly," he said once she had finished. "Adoption from Ukraine can be almost three times the cost of adopting from another country, even though you deal directly with the state authorities?" Alicia nodded. "Sounds a bit fishy to me," Eric responded. He paused before continuing. "I wouldn't have believed it possible for someone like Mr Thompson to charge as much as forty thousand dollars upfront on just a promise."

"Let me get a definite quote from him over the phone, I have his number." Alicia reached for her mobile phone and checked Roland's business card before dialling.

"Hello?" Roland answered after the third ring.

"Hi, this is Alicia Byrne. Am I interrupting anything?"

"No, not at all. What can I help you with?" Roland replied jovially.

Alicia explained that she had further discussed adoption with Adrian and that they had decided the option of adopting from Ukraine was one they wished to explore. "So, we would like to know how much is payable in advance," she concluded.

"I would require thirty thousand dollars since I need to make an initial deposit of twenty-five thousand. The rest contributes towards my own expenses," Roland said in a very syrupy voice.

"And how much of that will be refundable if we should desist from the process?" Alicia asked him once again.

"Fifteen thousand from the deposit, plus whatever is remaining after my expenses."

"OK, I'll speak with Adrian and get back to you shortly. Thank you for your time." She hung up and began explaining everything Roland had said to Eric.

"Hmm, so it'll be at least ten thousand on top of his expenses, which will definitely be the better part of five thousand because he'll obviously make it that way. Then there will be at least one exploratory trip to Kyiv…So, I'm guessing at least twenty initially. If you were to uncover a Moscow connection, I think that would be money well spent. As of now, we can't really tell what lies ahead…I'll have to mull it over and get back to you," he said. He took a few seconds to think before adding, "Now, first things first! What can I get for you?"

"A Jameson, please. Straight up." Alicia smiled while she ordered, and Eric gestured to the waiter that he wanted the same.

The next morning, Alicia woke up to find a text Eric had sent late at night: *Kyiv on. Pls let me have your a/c number.*

Alicia received a notification from her bank the following day, informing her that her account had been credited with thirty-five thousand dollars. She proceeded to make two calls, one to Roland and then one to Adrian, before texting her thanks to Eric.

Later that day, Alicia once again found herself in Yonkers at Roland Thompson's office. This time, her visit entailed going over the details of the contract and the next steps that needed to be taken.

"I suggest you fly with KLM via Amsterdam."

"Can you also recommend a hotel?"

"Yes, I can highly recommend either Riviera House or the smaller 11 Mirrors Design Hotel. They're both delightful."

"Well, I'm happy with the contract. Thank you." Alicia forced herself to smile throughout their interaction. She didn't feel comfortable with Roland since he seemed much too flaky to her. She had taken a permanent dislike to him.

"Splendid. Now you need to organise a marriage certificate. Perhaps your best option is the state of Virginia."

"How so?" Alicia asked.

"Well at only thirty bucks it's very inexpensive but more importantly, it's also extremely quick. All you need to do is simply travel to Virginia in the morning armed with a valid driving license. You'll be back in Manhattan that very afternoon as a married couple with a certificate to prove it."

"Sounds very romantic," Alicia said sarcastically.

"Perhaps not romantic but it is very practical. And you can always have a formal wedding blessing and reception at a later date."

"Yes, I guess," Alicia replied. "How will I get around in Kyiv?"

"You do not need to concern yourself with transportation. I will have people in situ to assist you. A man named Andre will pick you up at the airport. He speaks very good English.

Andre will drive you to your hotel and will also be available to accompany you to your meetings, which will have been arranged by a woman named Sofia. You will meet her shortly after you arrive in Kyiv."

"So, these people work for you?"

"Well, yes and no; they assist me on some occasions when needed but they are not full-time employees."

"And they can be trusted?" Alicia asked.

"Absolutely! I have used them on a number of occasions and have never received so much as a single complaint," he spoke with another sickly-sweet smile although his comment wasn't entirely true. Until recently, Roland had had all kinds of trouble when it came to finding reliable local assistance. Luckily, he had been approached and befriended by a man named Pavlov Andreiko. Since then, everything had gone smoothly.

Alicia suddenly realised she was running late for her doctor's appointment. She quickly signed the papers and gave Roland two cheques. One was for twenty-five thousand dollars, which would be placed in escrow. The other was for five thousand, which would cover Roland's expenses. After they shook hands, Alicia snapped up her signed set of documents and quickly excused herself. She waved goodbye to Betsy as she breezed through the reception area before leaving the building. Her deep intake of breath was the only indication of how relieved she was to be out of there.

Chapter XXII

The morning was warm and sticky, which meant that it was going to be a hot day in Kyiv. The city was feeling the impact of the Indian summer as the month of September was creeping in and the hot weather showed no sign of abating. Pavlov, who was strolling into his office, was already uncomfortable. He was using his newspaper to fan himself when he was greeted by Sofia, his assistant of over twenty years.

"I've just read an email that was sent overnight from Roland Thompson," she said without a smile or even a slight change of expression.

"More candidates for our precious little ones, I'm assuming?" Pavlov asked with a grin.

Sofia still didn't smile back and just relayed the message to him in a bland, nondescript way. "Somebody by the name of Alicia Byrne will be visiting shortly, and she's already made the first deposit."

"That's what we like to see, Sofia, so you could crack a smile. It wouldn't kill you, and you might even get a bonus this month." Sofia's only reply was a grimace and Pavlov laughed. "You're a hard-hearted woman, Sofia."

"Would you have me any other way, Pavlov?" This time she answered with a ghost of a smile.

"Never!" Pavlov declared as he pushed his office door open. "Bring me some coffee," he added before the door slammed shut.

Once Sofia had placed his coffee in front of him and left the room with another bang from the office door, Pavlov leaned back in his chair and rubbed his hands together. This latest deposit was the tenth this week, and he now had no doubt that the Magnitsky Act was going to be a great prospect for the future. What he did doubt, however, was Igor. At the moment Igor was happy but Pavlov knew from experience that this wouldn't last; Igor would get greedy. Igor always got greedy. And when he did, everyone suffered. *Soon he'll insist on charging fifty grand, then seventy, and so on and so on*, Pavlov thought bitterly to himself. His hatred for Igor was growing. It had started on the night of Liliya's murder and was growing in earnest with each passing day.

Pavlov shook his head, pushed himself up from his leather chair, and started pacing on the other side of his desk. His mind was racing with different images flashing in and out of his vision; Liliya's broken body as it lay crumpled on the floor, Liliya's long blonde hair, stained pink by her own blood, Liliya's dead eyes staring at him, following him, accusing him. Pavlov bowed his head and covered his face with his hands to stifle his screams. His mouth opened over and over again but not a sound escaped as he silently vented the rage and frustration that he held inside of him like a coiled snake. When he was finished, he ran his fingers through his hair and made his way around the desk. He slid back into his chair again.

Pavlov had decided that he needed to take action; the time had come for him to bring Igor down. He wanted his cousin dead, and he wanted Igor's position of status within the family to be his own. But more than anything, Pavlov wanted to hear Igor beg for his life just as he had heard Liliya beg for hers. Pavlov had heard her pleas for her life before hearing the crack of her skull when Igor had smashed it into the coffee table repeatedly. Pavlov knew the only way to silence the nightmares that haunted him was to avenge Liliya's death, and he made an oath to do this. He would kill Igor or die trying.

Chapter XXIII

Alicia and Adrian got back to Manhattan's Upper East Side just in time for their meeting with Eric. They had made plans to meet at the Regency Bar at Loews Regency Hotel, where Alicia had met Eric the last time they had spoken. But this time it was to celebrate their impromptu wedding, which had taken place earlier that day. Alicia and Eric were both excited whilst Adrian kept his unflappable cool as usual. After Eric had congratulated them and ordered three of the bar's signature martinis with blue cheese olives, he began discussing how to best take advantage of Alicia's forthcoming trip to Ukraine. It had been decided that she would go on her own to explore the landscape, which meant she was to find out as much about the adoption industry and who was on the receiving end of the significant profits involved.

Eric was particularly interested in whether or not the Russian authorities were, as he suspected, somehow involved. He had researched the subject at length and tried to summarise the scope of their investigation by focusing on the Magnitsky Act, or more precisely, the fallout that had followed it. He explained that the legislation was signed into law by President Obama in December 2012 and barred certain Russian officials who were suspected of human rights abuse from entering the USA. He described how the act permits the officials' funds that are kept in American banks to be frozen. The act also prohibits future trading with American financial institutions. Initially, eighteen Russian businessmen, all of whom had close ties to Vladimir Putin, were subject to the ban. By 2016, that number had risen to forty-four. "Moscow retaliated with an anti-Magnitsky law, the Dima Yakovlev Law, which, among other things, blocks American citizens from adopting from Russia.

"So, Alicia is going to Ukraine to investigate foreign law instead of adopting?" Adrian asked amusedly.

"Not exactly but I believe it is worth investigating whether or not there is a link between this and the recent spike in adoptions from Ukraine by Americans. More importantly, I want to know who, or what, this possible link might be. Presently, all I know is that huge sums of money are lining someone's pockets somewhere. I believe an unscrupulous person or organisation is trading in newborns." For Eric, this was a good enough reason to fund a further investigation into the abhorrent situation. If he lost the money, so be it, he was sure his pride would survive the financial loss. He ordered another round of drinks, this time to wish Alicia good luck.

Chapter XXIV

Alicia had just landed at Amsterdam Airport, Schiphol, after a pleasant and uneventful flight from JFK International Airport. In fact, she had managed several hours of sleep during the flight and felt both rested and upbeat. She searched the lists on the large electronic board for her connecting flight to Kyiv, which would be another flight with KLM. She was relieved to find that it was on time, due to board in an hour and a half. She decided to head for the gate and search for a café nearby.

Three lattes and two hours later, Alicia was finally seated on the plane and pleasantly surprised to find herself seated next to a young woman who looked to be in her early thirties. The woman smiled pleasantly at Alicia, indicating she had a friendly disposition. She was of small stature with a head of short, curly, red-blonde hair. She reminded Alicia of a young Meg Ryan.

Alicia decided to introduce herself. "Hi, I'm Alicia," she said, extending her hand.

"Hi, Miriam," the woman replied with an even broader smile as she took Alicia's outstretched hand. Alicia heard an accent that she couldn't place.

The conversation between the two women flowed from the moment their hands had touched. The plane wasn't full and the two of them were able to comfortably share a row of three seats with Alicia by the window and Miriam in the aisle seat. They used the empty spot between them to store small items such as their respective headphones, Miriam's sunglasses, a magazine, Alicia's crime novel by Jo Nesbo, plus a large bag of M&M's that Alicia had guiltily allowed herself to purchase during her layover. Alicia had immediately offered some to Miriam, who in turn retrieved a huge bag of marshmallows to contribute. The two of them snacked on the colourful sweets while chatting and giggling like teenage girls on a school trip.

Although born in Russia, it turned out that Miriam lived in Kyiv. She was on her way home after staying in Amsterdam for a bit of working and holidaying. She was a freelance journalist and fluent in Russian, French, and English, and she also knew a little bit of Hebrew. Her full name was Miriam Rivkin. She told Alicia that she wasn't married but did have a boyfriend in Amsterdam named Jurjen. "And what about you?" Miriam asked.

"I literally just got married!" Alicia exclaimed.

"And here you are, travelling on your own, without wearing a ring! Naughty you!" Miriam laughed.

Alicia blushed and went on to explain how she and Adrian had made a day trip to Winchester, Virginia, to obtain a marriage license quickly. She confided that they had been married in a rush in order to qualify for eventual adoption in Ukraine.

"That sounds even more intriguing and definitely calls for an explanation," Miriam said while laughing again.

Alicia began her story and told Miriam all about Adrian and how they had first met in Peru, which must have been fate as they were both from New York and lived close to one another. She explained their subsequent living arrangement of two adjacent apartments with a connecting door in Manhattan's Upper West Side. She also added that she and Adrian planned to have a proper wedding reception later in the year, which would include the exchange of rings.

"Wow!" Miriam exclaimed. "I'd love to write something about you two. Or better still, make a television show! I didn't know that a paralegal and an economist from the Big Apple could live such adventurous lives!"

They continued conversing and were on the best of terms by the time their lunch had arrived. It was in the form of a very tasty, slightly spicy, sandwich with a tiny, limp-looking side salad. They praised the Indonesian influence on Dutch cooking as they savoured their meal, each sipping on a cool glass of Heineken. Afterwards, Alicia ordered a neat Scotch.

"Whiskey after a meal?" Miriam asked, looking puzzled.

"Yep, that's how we like it." Alicia briefly explained her Irish heritage.

"So, you don't have any Ukrainian roots, then? Is this your first time visiting Ukraine?"

"Yes, it is!"

"So where in Kyiv will you be staying?" Miriam asked.

"Riviera House and 11 Mirrors have both been recommended to me, but I failed to make a reservation at either," Alicia admitted.

"I would definitely recommend 11 Mirrors. I mean, the Riviera House is a splendid hotel, but 11 Mirrors is so much more charming, you're going to love it! Their rooftop restaurant bar is one of the nicest spots in all of Kyiv."

Alicia made a mental note and thanked Miriam for the feedback. She was thrilled they had been seated together. "Any other recommendations?"

"Well, to be honest, I was actually wondering who is helping you with the adoption in Kyiv? I didn't want to ask because I didn't want to sound like an alarmist but...the country of Ukraine is very corrupt." Miriam looked genuinely concerned for Alicia.

Alicia told Miriam about Roland Thompson and Tomorrow Adoption Agency in Yonkers. She explained that Roland had contacts in Kyiv who were not only meeting Alicia at the airport but also assisting with any issues she might encounter involving the adoption process. She explained that there are no formal adoption agencies in Ukraine as the state and the courts handle these matters. "I'll probably have my first meeting with them tomorrow," she added.

"Could I give you my mobile number?" Miriam asked. "Just in case you need any further assistance while you're here?"

"That would be lovely!"

The two women continued talking until their plane landed. They then gathered their hand luggage and walked off the aircraft together. When it was time to part, they said their goodbyes with a hug and a kiss. After exchanging phone numbers, they had made plans to have dinner together that evening at the 11 Mirrors' rooftop venue. Alicia promised to call Miriam as soon as she checked in at the hotel.

After clearing immigration and customs, Alicia spotted a tall, dark, and exceedingly good-looking man. He was dressed in a tailored grey suit with a white dress shirt and a light blue tie. She was surprised to see her name written in black capital letters on the sign he was holding. She quickly approached the man, who presented himself as Andre. He took her luggage as she followed him to a large black Mercedes. He politely asked if her flight had been pleasant as he opened one of the back doors for her. All outside noise suddenly disappeared when Andre closed the door after her, causing Alicia to suspect the car might be armoured. She gave the window a small knock and confirmed she was right.

"Where to?" Andre asked.

"11 Mirrors Hotel," Alicia replied. She was pleasantly surprised by how firm yet polite her voice sounded. "But I don't have a reservation," she added.

"Not to worry, Mrs Byrne. That will be handled." Andre's voice was confident and business-like, and Alicia smiled at being called Mrs instead of Ms for the first time after her wedding ceremony.

True to his word, Andre followed Alicia to the reception desk once they had arrived at the hotel. He introduced her in English as a friend of Mr Pavlov Andreiko. The receptionist welcomed her to the hotel, promptly gave her a key to a single room with a queen-sized bed, and wished her a pleasant stay.

Andre carried her suitcase up to her room. Before leaving, he told her that he would return to pick her up at ten o'clock the following morning.

Once the gorgeous but very formal, Andre had left, Alicia checked the mini-bar and found a small bottle of Jonnie Walker. She emptied it into a glass, walked with it to the window, and pulled back the heavy, raspberry-coloured, velvet curtains. She stood there, taking in the beautiful view of Kyiv while sipping her whiskey. She felt on top of the world. A few minutes later, before unpacking, she called Miriam to finalise their plans for that evening.

Chapter XXV

Alicia was very much looking forward to the evening ahead. She had napped for a couple of hours and felt refreshed. Upon awakening, she texted Adrian and Eric and assured both that she had arrived safe and sound. After taking a hot shower, she contemplated what to wear on her first night out in Kyiv, finally deciding on a smart vintage cocktail dress. It was black and only slightly revealing since it was backless, and the lace trim hit her just below the knees. She paired it with teal kitten heels and wore her hair naturally.

She entered the rooftop bar at precisely eight-thirty in the evening and was immediately impressed by the stylish décor, which was quite a surprising upgrade when compared to her beloved Metro Bar that she frequented back home in New York. This place was extremely elegant and livelier, even though it was slightly smaller. It had a deep, rosy glow to it, and it was nearly packed, despite it being a weeknight. Alicia quickly spotted Miriam and joined her at a small, round, marble table for two.

As Alicia approached, Miriam stood up to greet her and the two hugged. "You look great!" Miriam exclaimed. She herself was wearing a violet silk blouse over scrubbed jeans and navy suede loafers.

"So do you!" Alicia replied truthfully. Both women had been dressed much more casually during their flight from Holland.

They ordered several different seafood dishes, one of which turned out to be Alicia's newfound favourite: crab served in the shell with the white and dark meat pulled out, mixed together, and topped with red caviar. They drank the delicious but potent local wine that Miriam had recommended. As the evening wore on, they accepted a few rounds of fancy cocktails from the male patrons of the establishment who had noticed the two women. Alicia wasn't usually much of a daiquiri drinker, but she thoroughly enjoyed what had been sent her way. She felt a bit naughty for accepting it but secretly loved the attention. *I should wear this dress more often*, she mused, remembering it had always been one of Adrian's favourites. She planned on calling him after dinner.

"So, when is your first appointment?" Miriam asked.

"I'm being picked up tomorrow morning at ten," Alicia replied.

"I was thinking, perhaps I could come with you? I mean, only if that would be all right with you. I am a little curious, I guess, and besides, I wouldn't want anything to happen to you."

Alicia, who was slightly nervous about attending alone, couldn't contain her relief. "Oh, how wonderful of you! I'm so pleased you're interested in coming with me!"

"I don't think that we should tell them I'm from Kyiv. I could be your Dutch friend for all they know. What do you think?"

"Sounds brilliant," Alicia said while raising her glass.

They toasted each other and, unbeknownst to them, resembled a pair of co-conspirators who had just agreed upon a strategic approach for meeting the opposition. After another bottle of wine accompanied by caviar and smoked salmon on blinis (a delicious and popular dish in Russia, similar to a pancake), they decided to call it a night. Alicia followed Miriam down to the reception area where they hugged and kissed goodnight, before agreeing to meet at ten o'clock the following morning.

Chapter XXVI

Andre and the large Mercedes were already waiting outside when Alicia and Miriam emerged from the hotel's main entrance the following morning. He exited the car, greeted Alicia, and held the door open for both women to enter. Once all of them were inside the car, Alicia introduced Miriam and they were promptly on their way. They had only travelled for a quarter of an hour before pulling up behind a large and quintessential-looking downtown building. Although the building had an elevator, they walked up two flights of stairs before entering a fairly large reception area. The receptionist took Alicia's passport and Miriam's identification card, which foiled their innocent plan of pretending she was originally from Holland. They were then led into a small but immaculate office, decorated with furniture and art pieces that were solely black and white, and were greeted by a middle-aged woman named Sonia.

"How pleasant to meet you, Mrs Byrne. How are you finding Kyiv so far?" Sonia spoke with a pleasant but unenthusiastic smile that made her cheery disposition seem feigned.

"Kyiv is splendid! This is my friend, Miriam, by the way." Alicia was going to add that they were new friends and had only just met on their flight from Amsterdam, but she imagined that might seem a little strange to Sonia. Alicia decided against admitting she had brought a woman she didn't really know to a very important meeting.

Thankfully, Sonia didn't take any interest in Miriam or her relationship with Alicia. "Well, welcome to both of you." Sonia wasted no time in opening a file on her desk that had Alicia's name written on the front of it. She quickly began to explain that they needed to hold on to Alicia's passport for a few hours because they needed to obtain a notarised copy for the adoption process. "But don't worry. You will have it back in just a few hours. I will see to it that Andre brings it to your hotel. I trust that you like 11 Mirrors? I think it's such a cute little hotel, and so central, don't you?"

"Yes, very much so," Alicia said automatically, absent-mindedly remembering the hotel's surroundings. The memory of seeing the Swedish Embassy suddenly struck her. It was situated almost directly opposite the hotel, and she had noticed it when Andre had driven them past it a short while ago. Alicia was distracted from her thoughts when a well-built, older gentleman entered the room. He spoke briefly with Sonia in Ukrainian before switching to English to introduce himself to Alicia and Miriam as Pavlov Andreiko. He then turned and left without shaking hands or saying goodbye.

"Back to business, then!" Sonia said in a forcibly upbeat way. She then tried a very rehearsed laugh so as not to sound too formal. "Would you like a boy or girl?"

Alicia was shocked by the speed at which this was going. She hadn't thought this was an option and so she hadn't discussed a preferred gender with Adrian. Without thinking, she said, "a boy." Thankfully, she managed to sound more convinced than she felt.

"Very good, we have several little boys." Sonia then explained that the babies were all in an orphanage in Donetsk, which was in eastern Ukraine. She also added that if Alicia wanted to see the baby before going through with the adoption, it would be necessary for her to travel there to see the child. "It is not the prettiest of places," she warned, "but you can fly there in the morning and be back in Kyiv by early evening on the same day."

Wow, this is moving way too fast! Alicia thought to herself in a panic. "Is that so?" she asked, buying herself some time to collect her thoughts and calm herself while Sonia spoke of all the good work Mr Andreiko was doing for the orphanage and the community.

As the meeting between the three women was taking place, two men had discretely left the office building. One of them was carrying Alicia's passport and was indeed on his way to the notary. The other man, however, was armed with a copy of Miriam's identification card and was on his way to confirm her identity and learn everything there was to know about Miriam Rivkin.

The meeting involving Sonia and the oblivious Alicia and Miriam had come to an end and the two women were preparing to leave, armed with a folder containing photos and basic background information on multiple baby boys who had been deemed healthy and available for adoption. Neither of the women had remembered to retrieve Miriam's identification card before departing, and they failed to remember it as Andre drove them back to the hotel either. As they ended their journey, Alicia observed once again how remarkably close the Swedish Embassy was, although she couldn't figure out why she had noticed in the first place, or why she thought this was noteworthy.

Chapter XXVII

As Andre was driving away and the pair were walking up to the hotel, Alicia looked at Miriam and said, "Well you're suspiciously quiet, aren't you? Hungry?"

Miriam looked deep in thought and spoke in a way that indicated she felt they had a lot of work to do. "Yes, but we have some serious business to attend to first. Let's go to your room, fire up your laptop, and brainstorm."

"That sounds good to me. Is something wrong?" Alicia nervously inquired.

"You bet. Let's move."

They were soon inside Alicia's room, which had been freshly made up. Alicia called the front desk and ordered room service, consisting of two burgers with fries and two Heinekens. Alicia grabbed two beers from the mini bar while they were waiting and handed one to Miriam, who was already hunkered down over Alicia's laptop.

"Just as I thought," Miriam exclaimed. "Pavlov Andreiko is exactly who I suspected."

"And who exactly is that?"

Miriam suddenly looked very serious and gravely concerned. She explained that Pavlov was one of the richest men in Ukraine. His fortune came from porn in all forms, including prostitution. As the 'King of Porn' in Ukraine, he had strong links to the Russian mafia, which controlled the sex industry worldwide. The fact that he was somehow involved with adoptions as well pointed directly to Russia and corruption in one form or another. "Furthermore," Miriam continued, "the orphanage is in Donetsk, which is virtually on the Russian border. The region has no effective border control and people wander freely between Ukraine and Russia," she concluded.

Now it was Alicia's turn to explain her interest in adopting from Ukraine. She divulged all the information she could to Miriam, including how she had initially sought information on the possibility of adoption because of her age, and the fact that she had not yet had a successful pregnancy, and only had one kidney. She explained that she was still considering pregnancy but hadn't ruled out adoption entirely. Finally, she told Miriam about Eric and the Behaviour Society community. She confided in Miriam that they had footed the bill for her Ukrainian adoption for investigative purposes since Eric believed that Russia was somehow connected to the recent increase in foreign adoptions from Ukraine.

As it turned out, Miriam was familiar with the Magnitsky Act and the Kremlin's subsequent response to it. "So that's the big picture, or should we say macro situation? What we're investigating now is a micro detail; a mega rich man involved with porn who has clear ties to the Russian mob. We now know he is directly involved with adoptions as well and is using an orphanage that is situated in the most lawless part of Ukraine, right on the Russian border. So, how well connected is your friend?"

"Eric is extremely well connected," Alicia replied.

"With large media outlets, like papers or magazines or broadcasting stations?"

"All of the above."

The women looked at each other and smiled mischievously, both knowing exactly what to do.

Several hours later, both Alicia and Miriam were satisfied with their lunch of burgers, beers, and more importantly, their lengthy report for Eric. The report, without mentioning Pavlov Andreiko's name, outlined in great detail how the adoptions started from orphanages in the city of Donetsk and how the region's current conditions made it very conducive for any kind of activity that might not be considered above board. Their finished written work also included the fact that it would be nearly impossible to prove if the babies were of Russian birth instead of Ukrainian, that it was possible lots of money was involved, that Ukraine had no adoption agencies by law, and that it was simply a judge who ultimately signed the permit. Furthermore, their report highlighted that neither Ukraine nor Russia were signatories of the Hague Convention. The new friends had carefully drafted the document with enough circumstantial evidence but without any solid proof. They wrote to Eric that they intended to include that later once their investigation had uncovered more.

After emailing the document to Eric, it was almost seven o'clock in the evening. Both Alicia and Miriam were exhausted but excited and satisfied with their work. They left the room and headed for the rooftop bar, where they ordered a large whisky each, straight up.

After another drink or two with Miriam, Alicia was back in her room and saw the black dress she had worn yesterday hanging over the back of a chair. She realised at that moment that she hadn't called Adrian last night as she had intended to.

In fact, she had only texted him once since she had arrived in Kyiv. She thought it best to call him immediately, although she was slightly tipsy.

After another beer from the hotel room's mini fridge, while divulging everything that had happened since she had boarded her flight to Ukraine, Alicia was delivering a fierce and righteous monologue on the rights of the orphans in Donetsk even though her audience was only Adrian. He was trying his best to follow her. "Well, it's a good thing we're still considering conceiving," Adrian tried to add in. "How are prospective mothers supposed to make an informed decision? The specialist doctors only seem to care about the health of the mother. What about the risks involving the fetus, the child?" Adrian was trying to sound serious and engaged. "Hmm," he said, and he continued to say it whenever Alicia took a brief pause to recover her breath. Other than that, he said nothing. He was having difficulty deciphering what Alicia wanted and decided that maybe, just maybe, all she really wanted at that moment was to speak with him. When she suddenly paused for a little longer, Adrian knew that her rant was over and quickly gathered his thoughts. *Be supportive,* he thought. "I can totally see where you're coming from, and I completely agree with you." He was pleased with his carefully chosen words. Alicia had sounded bewildered but was calmed by hearing this. She felt peace wash over her, and she felt loved. *He is a real man, and he's my man,* she thought. "I miss you." She sighed.

"I wish I could pour you a drink," Adrian said, knowing it would make her smile. "What time is it there?"

Alicia hadn't considered the time until he had asked. "Not quite midnight," she said, looking at the clock on the bedside table.

"What are you wearing?"

Alicia couldn't help but giggle. "I was wearing that black dress you like last night."

"In that case, I'll just imagine you're still wearing it. Would you like to have a drink with me?"

Although it was just another tiny bottle of Johnnie Walker from the mini-bar, Alicia thought it was even better than the expensive stuff she had been sipping on upstairs. They continued talking until she couldn't keep her eyes open any longer. The two said goodnight and she fell fast asleep.

Chapter XXVIII

A man was sitting in his van with a newspaper in his lap. It was early in the morning, and he was watching the front entrance of Miriam's building, waiting for her to emerge.

Sure enough, Miriam came through the front door and hurried over to her Vespa a moment later, getting into it and speeding away. The man waited another ten minutes before getting out of his vehicle. He was dressed in workman's overalls and completed the look with a safety helmet and steel-toed boots. He opened the back of the van and retrieved an expandable aluminium ladder. He carried it over his right shoulder as he made his way to the side of the building. He effortlessly expanded the ladder, leaned it against the building, and swiftly climbed the short distance to Miriam's second-floor balcony. After hopping over the railing, the man lifted the ladder, folded it up, and placed it on the balcony floor. The door was slightly ajar, fixed by an elastic band and a rubber doorstopper pushed underneath from the inside. He removed his footwear and headgear and left them beside the ladder. He was indoors within seconds before anyone saw him.

Once inside, he found himself in the main living space of the small apartment. A framed opening to his right revealed a small kitchen and served as evidence that there had once been a door there, no doubt removed years ago to prioritise space.

The main room didn't resemble a living room so much but rather a combined workspace and eating space with a little sitting area in front of a large television screen. It was not suitable for entertaining guests but was certainly a comfortable enough space for one or two people. He could see the bedroom through another framed yet doorless entrance at the other end of the open-plan room. He quickly made his way through the whole place, inspecting every inch of it as he went. He also verified that the front door was bolted. He had expected as much, which meant he would need to leave the same way he had entered.

He knew very well what he was looking for, and he was sure he had lots of time at his disposal. He noticed that the computer on the desk had been left on, so he decided to start there. The screen was black; he clicked the return key, and the screen came alive, displaying a smiling couple and a small window asking for a password. He held up the keyboard, which was neither new nor extensively used, against the light and expertly searched the keys, finding one that stood out as being frequently used. On a whim, he pressed the number 1 and then the return key again. He was in, and it had been easier than he had imagined. After only fifteen minutes of reading Miriam's emails and scrolling through her address book, he made a call on his phone.

After repeating the information he had retrieved, he was disappointed when the voice on the other end confirmed his mission was complete. The man would have liked to stay and get 'better acquainted', something that for him meant the use of violence, with the pretty woman who lived here.

Chapter XXIX

Alicia woke up and quickly noticed she was very hungry and slightly hungover. She started to reconstruct the previous day's events in her head, soon recalling her encounter with Andre, Sonia, and Pavlov and their offices. She also remembered she had spent the rest of the day with Miriam, eating lunch while writing the report for Eric before going upstairs to the roof and getting drunk. She had stayed up later than she had anticipated speaking with Adrian and hadn't eaten anything besides the burger and fries, hence her hunger.

She got up to check her computer before ordering breakfast. There was an email from Eric:

Alicia, many thanks for such a detailed and fascinating report. Well Done!!! I am handing this over to a friend of mine at the NYT but without mentioning your name. Keep up the good work, be careful, and let me know if you need anything. I would advise you to start considering your return if you haven't already. I don't expect you to go to Donetsk. (Nor would I want you to go there alone!) Lots of love, Eric.

There was also a footnote for her to contact Eric's good friend if she found herself in need. His friend's name was Betty Unger, who worked at the US Embassy in Kyiv. Eric had included her office number, address, and her personal mobile number.

She read his message twice and copied Betty's full name and contact details onto the hotel's complimentary notepad. She ripped off the top page so that she could always carry the information with her. She thought of folding the small piece of paper and tucking it into her passport only to realise she didn't have her passport. She called reception to see if there was an envelope for her. When she was informed there wasn't, she searched for Sonia's business card and called her.

"Good morning, Alicia," Sonia answered pleasantly. "What can I do for you? Do you want me to book you a trip to Donetsk?"

"Good morning, Sonia. Actually, I still have to speak with my husband about that." Alicia had discussed Donetsk with Adrian but had not mentioned visiting the place since she had no intention of doing so. "I will get back to you on that matter as soon as I can. I'm calling because I'm wondering where my passport is. It wasn't delivered to the hotel yesterday."

"That surprises me. Let me make some calls to see what has happened. But please, don't you worry, I will call you straight back."

Sonia called back two minutes later and said that they had not managed to obtain a notarised copy yesterday. She didn't know for what reason but said that it would most definitely be done that morning. She assured Alicia that she would have her passport shortly after lunch.

Alicia was just coming out of the shower when the phone rang again. "Hello?"

"Alicia, this is Miriam. I am on my way over to take you out for breakfast and then some sightseeing! After today, you will have seen all the wonderful things Kyiv has to offer." She sounded upbeat and obviously didn't share Alicia's hangover.

Luckily, Alicia hadn't ordered room service yet, so she promised to be ready and downstairs in less than ten minutes. First, she dried her hair with a towel, as best she could, twisted it up into a wet bun, and called Eric to give him an update.

Chapter XXX

Igor was already in Pavlov's office when the report on a Ukrainian named Miriam Rivkin was delivered. While Pavlov was deep in thought about the report's contents, Igor was livid and flying off the handle. "A fucking freelance journalist? A fucking international and bilingual freelance journalist? That's all we fucking needed!" He couldn't stop screaming.

Early the next morning, when a certain *New York Times* article was sent to him electronically by a contact, even Pavlov understood that immediate action was desperately required. Although unwilling to admit it, he hoped for Alicia's sake that he would be the one tasked with dealing with her. He hoped Igor's men wouldn't be involved with the intervention or worse, Igor himself.

Chapter XXXI

Jurjen de Vries was heading home after a night out with some friends in Amsterdam. It was just after midnight, and he was cycling along the canal. He could see his apartment on the other side of the water as he had left the light on in the living room. This was a custom of his since he didn't like stepping into the dark once he returned home in the evenings. In this respect, Jurjen was not an extreme environmentalist. Since he lived an environmentally friendly life otherwise, he thought that this tiny indulgence was nothing to be ashamed of. Instead of breaking, he simply stopped pedalling and glided a short distance while balancing on one of his pedals with his left foot and swooping his right leg over the back wheel. He was leaning on the handlebars and resting on one side of his bike as it slowed to a stop. He hopped off the pedal he had been standing on and walked across the narrow bridge. Reaching the other side, he was close enough to his apartment to just continue walking. He stopped briefly and lit a cigarette.

Just as he had started smoking and walking again, Jurjen heard somebody from behind him calling out his name. He turned around and faced a man who was approaching him. "Jurjen de Vries?" the man repeated with an indistinguishable accent.

"Yes?" Jurjen replied.

Suddenly, before Jurjen could get a good look at whoever was addressing him, everything went black. The man had administered a karate chop over Jurjen's neck, and Jurjen promptly collapsed, dropping his freshly lit cigarette and falling over his bike. The man picked Jurjen and his bike up and moved both over to the dark side of the street. He threw the bike away and started administering some hard blows to different parts of Jurjen's body, kicking and punching him. His orders were not to kill but to severely injure Jurjen, just badly enough for several days of hospitalisation. The man knew exactly how to achieve this and started by breaking several of Jurjen's ribs with enough force that it would result in some mild internal bleeding. He then made certain Jurjen's face was severely bruised and that the skin was bust open on the corner of his brow and upper lip.

After the man was satisfied, he removed the cash and credit cards from Jurjen's wallet but made sure to leave the cards with photos on them so that Jurjen could be identified. He left the badly beaten body by the bike and used Jurjen's mobile phone to report the attack. He then left the phone by the body and walked briskly into the night.

Chapter XXXII

After another night in Kyiv, Alicia woke up early. She checked her computer and found a copy of an article in that day's *New York Times*, one that contained the story of a possible Russian connection to the adoptions in Ukraine and thus the circumvention of the fallout that had followed the Magnitsky Act. The article went further than the report she had complied with Miriam and only Eric Holstein of Behaviour Society was quoted. Her passport had not yet been returned but it was still too early to call Sonia. Alicia had a shower and got dressed.

Alicia's phone rang shortly after she had showered. It was Miriam, and she was hysterical as she informed Alicia that her boyfriend had been attacked. "Jurjen was mugged and badly beaten last night. He is in hospital with several broken ribs, a concussion, and internal bleeding. I'm heading for the airport to catch the next flight to Amsterdam. The agency still has my identification card, I have my passport so I'll just pick up the card when I get back. Be very careful, Alicia. I'll call you once I am by Jurjen's side."

Alicia was in shock. Could this somehow be linked to the *NYT* article and what she and Miriam were investigating? *No, that's too farfetched*, she reasoned with herself. *Besides, the article had only just been published.* But the words from

Miriam about being careful echoed through her head. Without Miriam, she was on her own.

However, attracted by the beautiful morning, Alicia decided to take a short walk around the area of her hotel to search for a coffee shop. She passed by the Swedish Embassy and admired the beauty of Kyiv. Its multiple, majestic church towers proudly rose above the surrounding picturesque architecture.

After a delicious café latte, Alicia decided to head back to her hotel. Upon reaching the main entrance, Alicia saw a large black Mercedes Benz parked outside the hotel. It looked exactly like the one Andre drove. Sure enough, once she was inside the lobby, Alicia spotted his familiar face. He was standing in front of the reception desk and nodded respectfully in her direction.

Alicia walked up to him. "Hello, Andre. I wasn't expecting you."

"I have come to return your passport," Andre said as he handed it to her. "I was just about to leave it here at the front desk so I wouldn't disturb you."

Alicia thanked him. *What a coincidence and a relief*, she thought to herself. She watched Andre leaving and realised she was hungry. The clock over the reception desk confirmed that it was indeed time for lunch. She felt like having something French and a member of staff recommended a traditional bistro called Très Français.

Alicia took a taxi from the hotel and was soon there. *What a lovely place*, she thought to herself as she eyed the charming old restaurant. It was relatively busy but she managed to get a small table inside. She ordered snails as a starter and asked the sommelier for a full bottle of their best Côtes du Rhône.

She had two glasses with the snails and had just asked for a recommendation of a substantial main course when she spotted Pavlov Andreiko walking into the restaurant. He was accompanied by a much younger man. It was clear Pavlov hadn't spotted her, and she was glad of this because she had no wish to bring her presence to his attention. She ate her boeuf bourguignon with gusto and finished her wine. She didn't want to linger in case it meant being noticed by Pavlov, so she decided to have coffee or dessert back at the hotel. She asked for the bill and a taxi left a nice tip and exited. It was her father who had taught her how to tip. "Alicia," he said, "always tip generously if you intend on coming back to a place. Otherwise, don't bother at all."

Once she was back at the hotel, Alicia ordered coffee and brandy to her room. Half an hour later, she crawled up under a blanket and fell fast asleep.

Chapter XXXIII

Alicia awoke a couple of hours later with a raging headache. She swallowed two pills and went to the bathroom to splash cold water on her face. After applying minimal makeup, she checked her phone but still hadn't received any message from Miriam. She headed out for the nearby coffee shop. Once seated with another large café latte in front of her, she asked if she could also have a brandy. The man behind the counter smiled and suddenly disappeared. He popped back up with a bottle, which he evidently kept underneath the counter, and poured Alicia a large brandy into a ceramic mug. "No licence," he explained. She smiled back, grateful for his defiance.

Once back at the hotel, she came upon Andre in the lobby yet again. She couldn't quite believe her eyes. Feeling a bit tipsy, she joked, "Andre, we just can't go on meeting like this."

Andre, who didn't quite understand, replied, "Excuse me, Mrs Byrne, but I am here to drive you to a meeting you must attend. Mr Andreiko has asked me to come and collect you."

"Where?" Alicia asked suspiciously, wary of the fact that Pavlov wanted a last-minute meeting.

"It is at another one of Mr Pavlov's business locations."

Deciding she didn't really have a choice in the matter, Alicia replied, "I need to pick up my jacket and will be downstairs shortly." When she got to her room, she tried but failed to contact Miriam to check on her. She collected her jacket and left.

Ten minutes later, Alicia was seated in the backseat of the comfortable vehicle and looking out the window. The car was apparently on the motorway and heading out of Kyiv. She began to feel even more anxious and puzzled when the car swung off the main highway and onto a small road. They were heading towards what looked like a dense forest.

"We are about to arrive," said Andre, who had noticed her apparent uneasiness.

"I was just about to ask," Alicia replied as she saw a castle-like mansion coming into view. "What a place!" she exclaimed, and Anton explained that it was one of Mr Pavlov's principal businesses.

It was nearly evening but the sun was still up. The courtyard was overflowing with expensive-looking cars. As Alicia stepped into the reception area, she was surprised to hear live rock music coming from what appeared to be a restaurant or bar located to the left of the main entrance. She was met by a younger man, and it happened to be the man she had seen with Pavlov at Très Français. He escorted her into a beautiful office with antique furniture and art to match. He introduced himself as Igor and motioned for her to sit on the sofa while he took a seat in an adjacent armchair.

"Where is Pavlov?" Alicia asked.

"Pavlov will not be joining us," Igor coolly replied, handing her a printed copy of the now-infamous article that described alleged Russian connections to adoptions in Ukraine. Although she had not been directly quoted in the article, it was clear the material used had been based on her reportage with Eric Holstein.

"Have you read this article?" inquired Igor.

"No, I have not," Alicia lied while trying to look at it curiously and innocently as if for the first time.

"In that case, I would urge you to read it. It is my understanding that the information is based on feeds coming from you," Igor said smoothly.

"I'm not sure what you mean," Alicia lied again.

"But of course you do," Igor replied in a tone that was not friendly but not quite harsh.

"You're making me uncomfortable." It was the only honest response Alicia could think of.

"And this article makes me very uncomfortable, so I believe it may be time for you to leave Ukraine," Igor said. "Perhaps a short holiday to see parts of Russia could be an option," he added.

"I want to leave now." Alicia tried standing up as she spoke, but Igor was quick to push her back down on the sofa. "Don't touch me," she managed to say meekly once she was seated again.

"You must be dealt with, Mrs Byrne. Or is it Mrs Franks now?" This stranger somehow knew Adrian's family name, which made Alicia even more alarmed than she already was. "You will retract the information you have given to your contact in America," Igor continued. "Perhaps right away, or after a trip to my beloved Russia. I personally will decide your arrangements, and one option includes approximately a dozen well-built Russian men who will make certain you'll have a Russian baby once they're through with you. It would be a sort of semi-adoption since you won't know who exactly the father is. I hope you are strong enough to survive until your pregnancy since twelve strong Russian males with vivid imaginations can be…how shall I put it? Somewhat exhaustive."

"Anything but that," whispered Alicia as she felt a cold sweat building up at the back of her neck. She didn't even notice she was crying.

"So, Olga it is!" Igor announced while cheerfully clapping his hands together. A stern-looking and athletically built woman suddenly entered the office through a backdoor Alicia hadn't noticed. She had blonde hair pulled back into a tight knot and wore large round glasses with thin metal frames. She was dressed in all black.

"Alicia, meet Ms Olga Karluk," Igor said. "Olga, you will be assisting Mrs Byrne twenty-four-seven for as long as it takes. She has some very important reports to write."

As they were leaving the mansion, Alicia noticed Olga was carrying a suitcase. In the car, Olga had seated herself beside Alicia in the backseat. The drive back to the hotel was quick, tense, and silent. When they arrived, Andre and Olga were close to either side of Alicia as they escorted her indoors. Andre looked indifferent and Alicia found his features harsh and no longer attractive. She was hardly surprised to hear the receptionist greeting them on their way in, welcoming all of them as if he had expected her and her guests at that very moment. "I see you have company, Mrs Byrne, so your new suite will be ready momentarily. We are just in the process of moving your belongings." He smiled before addressing the bellboy. "Please help Ms Karluk with her suitcase."

Chapter XXXIV

Eric was rereading Alicia's latest report, and he found himself surprised and disappointed. Unlike the earlier report, this one was short and read as if it had been written in a rush. The brief content basically stated a second report was to follow, one that would effectively retract all previous allegations of a Russian connection. It was also going to deny the existence of the corrupt system that was circumventing the repercussions of the Magnitsky Act. He reasoned that either Alicia had initially been wrong, or she was, for some reason, fighting to undo what she had initially put in motion. But if so, why? Was Alicia somehow in trouble because of what she had written? Was it possible that the poor girl had found herself in more danger? He knew that it was his responsibility to check up on her. He decided to look at flights from New York to Kyiv if he or Adrian should need to travel to Alicia.

After realising just how cumbersome it was for him to fly to Kyiv, Eric decided to call Alicia. After repeated attempts of trying to reach her by phone or email, he called Adrian. It turned out that Adrian had had no problems keeping in touch with Alicia, who had called and texted regularly. Speaking to Eric, Adrian realised he hadn't spoken with Alicia in the last two days. He admitted this was odd now that he was thinking about it, and he hadn't noticed until now since he had been so busy with work. Eric, who didn't want to alarm Adrian, said he was getting periodical updates; a half-true statement at best. He suddenly had an idea, flowers. Yes, of course. Flowers.

Barbara was pleasantly surprised when she found a voice message from Eric asking her to call him back at her earliest convenience. She dialled his number immediately.

"Hello, Barbara. Thanks for calling back so quickly." Eric spoke warmly and enquired if she was free for lunch. They agreed to meet uptown at Park Avenue Café.

Eric, always the gentleman was ten minutes early. He immediately spotted Barbara as she entered the restaurant which is situated just below street level. He stood up and kissed her on both cheeks and offered her a glass of red wine, which Barbara readily accepted. "What a surprise," Barbara gushed. She thought the restaurant was not only suitably posh but also quaint, and Eric always made her feel inexplicably giddy.

"Catching up," Eric replied in a most jovial way.

"Two attractive blondes just catching up, are we?" Barbara asked rhetorically, trying to flirt with him.

"Just catching up," repeated Eric in a non-committal way.

Sitting down, looking at the menu, they both made their choices from the large selection of 'signature sandwiches' which went well with what they were drinking. After they had a second glass of red to finish up their meals, Eric asked for the cheque. He didn't want to linger. He waited until they were about to stand up and part ways before asking Barbara for a favour.

"But of course, Eric. What can I do for you?"

"I need you to do the following," Eric replied, grabbing a clean napkin and writing on it while he continued speaking.

"I need you to call a florist in Kyiv and send a bouquet of twelve red roses to the 11 Mirrors Design Hotel, for Alicia, with a card that reads, 'Remembering our night in Puno.' Can you do that?"

"What do you mean? Alicia and I didn't even go to Puno, and although I could perhaps do her a few…small favours, I am, as you probably know, leaning more towards the other team. And, since you know Adrian, you know she is, too."

She is hopeless, Eric thought to himself. "Indeed, indeed. But Alicia has been recently unavailable and was acting a bit strangely when she managed to get in touch through reporting. I'm worried that she could be in some kind of trouble."

"Do you think it's possible she's been kidnapped yet again?" Barbara's dry tone suggested she believed this was impossible.

"I don't know, I'm just worried, I guess. It's probably nothing. But would you mind doing this anyway? Are you game?"

"Of course, as always." Barbara's shameless and flirty attitude was back. Eric made a call on his mobile and spoke briefly to somebody on the other end before handing the phone over to Barbara.

"Hi, my name is Barbara Shuler, and I would like to send a dozen red roses to a friend in Kyiv, Ukraine. Her name is Alicia Byrne, B-Y-R-N-E, and the address is…" She looked down and gave the address on the paper napkin that Eric had just slid over to her on the table. Unbeknownst to Barbara, she had just spoken with Betty Unger, the second in command at the US embassy in Kyiv. Without disconnecting, she handed the phone back to Eric.

"Yes, see you soon and the very best to you as well my dear," Eric said before ending the call.

Once outside, Eric gave Barbara a warm embrace and kissed her on both cheeks before heading to an awaiting car that was already carrying his luggage. He was heading for JFK and his private charter was destined for Kyiv.

Chapter XXXV

Alicia was in the bathroom and finally alone, although she could hear Olga moving about in the hotel suite from behind the closed door. She felt weak, terrified and was frequently pretending she had to use the toilet to regain her composure. She wished desperately that Barbara was there with her. Surely Barbara would stand up to the dreadful Ms Karluk.

Alicia could see no way out of her current situation and knew she was trapped. Who would be able to come to her rescue? Nobody. She didn't know anyone who would be able to help her except Miriam, and although Miriam was the closest and most likely solution, she was all the way in Amsterdam. This was not a simple nightmare from which Alicia could suddenly awake and escape. A cold tingle crept down her spine and added to her terror. She kept telling herself that Igor only needed her to redact her story about the Russian connection to the Ukraine adoptions and she would then be allowed to go free. Alicia somehow doubted it would be that simple, however. She couldn't shake the image of multiple men tossing her around effortlessly like a toy while plotting how to best take advantage of their sex slave.

Alicia knew she would never be able to overpower Olga. Could she somehow befriend her instead? She finally decided to confront Olga with an air of false easiness and comprehension. Alicia's Irish upbringing decided it for her.

She told herself she was strong as she desperately tried to convince the image of herself in the bathroom mirror to carefully open the door. She immediately came face to face with Olga's strong stature. Olga looked down on Alicia with dull eyes. There was no compassion to be had from those eyes, and Alicia cowered slightly as she tried to pass Olga and enter the room. Olga took Alicia by the neck and tilted her wrist forward, forcing Alicia's chin slightly backwards so she had to face Olga's emotionless gaze. She had no interest in Alicia feeling anything but fear.

"I don't feel sorry for you, and I am not here to make it easy for you." Her English was remarkably flawless, and her words sent another chill down Alicia's nearly numb spine.

"What exactly do you want from me?" Alicia managed to ask but without strength or confidence.

"I don't want anything from you. Hell, I don't even know you! The only thing I know that I can tell you is that you are in deep shit. I also know what Igor does to women for his own amusement, and you certainly don't look like a survivor to me."

Alicia felt even weaker than she had before. Her legs sagged under her, forcing her into a kneeling position. Olga just looked down on her with what could have been a mild look of disgust or disinterest. Alicia decided that trying to read Olga was a fool's errand, and so was attempting to get any sympathy from her. Alicia knew with certainty that she wasn't getting out of this.

Chapter XXXVI

Olga heard the knock on the hotel room's door. It was flowers for Alicia, who was again in the bathroom.

"You've got twelve red roses with a card here. It's from somebody named Barbara, referring to a special night in a place called Puno," Olga barked at Alicia as she emerged from her morning shower.

"Hmm," Alicia said while she read the card. For a moment she was puzzled; she hadn't accompanied Barbara and their friend Luisa to Puno while they were all in Peru, but she tried not to let it show. Then she had the sudden realisation that it must be Eric's way of trying to reach out to her. *He is ingenious*, she thought as a warm feeling came over her. She had been missing in action, but Eric had found her.

"No need to blush," Olga said.

"Hmm," Alicia repeated trying to give nothing away as she gathered her thoughts and straightened her posture.

Breakfast arrived shortly after the flowers, and the two ate in relative peace considering the tension in the room was high. Alicia had her confidence back, but she didn't dare show it. Thanks to the flowers and the cryptic message, she knew help was on the way.

Following breakfast, Olga sat Alicia down in front of her laptop to work on some more material that would be sent to Eric. It was for him to send to *The New York Times* as a retraction of the inflammatory article about Russian babies being smuggled across the border and put up for adoption in Ukraine.

Chapter XXXVII

Corporal Luchenko was sitting at his desk in his small office in the Kremlin. The only natural light was through a small window high up, just below the ceiling. He had a copy of *The New York Times* opened in front of him, revealing the article 'Russian Adoptions through Ukraine'. The article quoted several different sources but only one was named: Eric Holstein of Behaviour Society. The article outlined in great detail that Russian babies were being smuggled to Ukraine and placed in orphanages for adoption by American citizens and other foreigners.

It was Luchenko's task to see to it that this inflammatory article, which had its roots in Kyiv through an American by the name of Alicia Byrne, was taken care of. His task wasn't exactly clear yet, and it was apparently coming from the very top, possibly from Commander Putin himself. Unfortunately, it had been necessary to contact the *Bratva*, the Russian brotherhood. Luchenko was now awaiting an update from somebody known to him only as Igor, who was already in Kyiv dealing with the situation. Thus far, the only news he had received from Igor was that the plan was still in the making, and he found this particularly irritating.

Chapter XXXVIII

Alicia had finally completed the task that had been forced upon her. She leaned back with difficulty from stiff muscles and sheer exhaustion and looked on painfully desperately as Olga read through the new script.

"Well, this reads pretty well to me," Olga finally said. "Now, that wasn't so difficult, was it?" Olga spoke in a condescending schoolteacher's voice while she patted Alicia's head with a bit too much force. "Let's see what Igor thinks, shall we?" She attached the document to an email and sent it. Her mobile rang less than ten seconds after her final click of the mouse. She answered and without saying anything, motioned Alicia back to the computer with a single sharp snap of her fingers. Once Alicia had flung her body forwards and had her hands hovering over the keyboard, Olga repeated a few corrections aloud that were being dictated to her over the phone. She disconnected the call without saying anything else and joined Alicia. Together they reread what was displayed on the screen and finished the text. Olga then sent the document to Alicia's own computer and oversaw Alicia sending it to Eric.

"Now cheer up and put on some decent clothes," Olga said to Alicia. "We're going upstairs for a drink and a bite to eat."

Alicia was reluctant but obliged, resolving that she was at least glad to be finally getting out of the room. She decided to take a quick shower and put on some makeup since she worried that she looked as terrible as she felt. She soon emerged from the bathroom and found Olga had put on fresh clothes as well but was still wearing all black. Olga's bed, which had been propped up against the door to prevent Alicia from escaping during the night, was now back in its rightful place. The two-headed out but only as far as the rooftop bar and restaurant. Olga seemed pleased with herself, and Alicia tried her best to look normal. She nodded at the bartender who seemed to recognise her since he had smiled at her.

As the evening wore on, live music started, and she began to notice that Olga was quite the heavy drinker. She seemed to know how to hold her liquor though, so Alicia didn't hold on to the hope that her babysitter would suddenly become incogitant of their present circumstances. The food looked exquisite, but Alicia didn't have an appetite and found herself unable to taste what little food she had managed to swallow. She tried convincing herself that Olga was Miriam, and they were just two friends out for the evening, but it was no use.

When Olga got into a conversation with a couple at the next table, Alicia saw her chance. She stood up and excused herself as casually as she could, saying she needed to use the ladies' room. When Olga seemed to hesitate ever so slightly, Alicia didn't wait. She headed straight for the restrooms and tried to relieve herself, thinking this might be her last chance to do so before she bolted. When she exited the bathroom, she dashed straight to the bar and hunkered down behind it. Once behind the bar and sitting on the floor, Alicia held out a one-hundred-dollar bill with pleading eyes to the man who had smiled at her. "Help me, please. I'm in grave danger," she whispered to the surprised bartender.

The bartender didn't hesitate. He took her money and, in a flash, managed to clear an old mixer, some empty buckets used for icing bottles of wine, and a few other things from directly underneath the bar. He looked at Alicia and pointed to the empty space without saying anything. Alicia knew to move into it and quickly crawled in and curled up, trying to make herself as small as possible.

Olga was getting nervous but most of all, she was extremely angry. She got up while the couple she had been speaking with was in the middle of asking her a question about Kyiv. Without excusing herself and blatantly ignoring them, she set off to search the entire top floor. She checked their room twice. She harassed every member of staff she could find but not one of them had seen Alicia. Everyone at reception swore they never saw her come through the lobby. Olga knew that Igor was not going to be pleased but she knew she needed to call him and the sooner, the better. She needed reinforcements. At least the retraction he so desperately wanted had been accomplished, approved, and sent. However, having Alicia on the loose meant she could potentially jeopardise the whole thing, so Olga knew that finding Alicia was a priority. She reluctantly called Igor to tell him the bad news.

Igor was livid and immediately sent two men to the hotel to help with the search for Alicia. One of the men relieved Olga at the door of the bar to check everybody exiting. The other searched everywhere else with Olga. Receptionists, servers, and other staff members were interviewed along with the regular taxi drivers but there had been no sign of Alicia.

Since her computer and passport were in her room, it was clear that she hadn't been there. It was as if she had gone up in smoke.

The bar was closing. After the last guests had left, the man at the door made a thorough and final search of the place. At one point, Alicia could see his shoes and part of his trousers as he walked behind the bar to interview the bartender. They spoke Ukrainian, so Alicia had no idea what they were discussing. Once the bar had been cleaned and the remaining staff members had left, the bartender crouched down and peered inside at Alicia. He motioned for her to come out. She was stiff and found it painful to untangle herself. She slowly stood up.

"They're looking everywhere for you," the bartender said. "I don't think it's safe for you to leave. You better sleep here until I come back and open up tomorrow morning. Come with me and I'll show you where you can rest." He led her to a small windowless room that seemed to be a storage area for bar supplies. He started shifting boxes of wine and spirits around and produced a mattress. He explained to Alicia that he had slept there before on rare occasions. Alicia decided not to imagine what those rare occasions might have been and instead admired his craftiness. He placed the mattress next to the wall and built a wall of boxes around it so that both the mattress and the person sleeping on it would be completely shielded from anyone who walked in. Before he left, he gave Alicia a large bowl of nuts and raisins, plus two half-empty cartons of orange juice. She was grateful for his thoughtfulness.

"I'll lock the door for your safety and will be back tomorrow morning."

"Goodnight, and thanks for helping me," Alicia murmured. She had dropped to her knees and was about to curl into a ball when she stopped the kind stranger before he left. "I'm Alicia, by the way," she said.

"Yes, well, I know." He chuckled hesitantly. "Everyone knows your name now that they have all of us looking for you." Even though she should've guessed it, Alicia felt ill at hearing this development now that she had been able to catch her breath and collect her thoughts. "My name is Freddy," the bartender added.

"Thank you, Freddy." Alicia barely managed to choke out the words since tears had finally started pooling in her eyes. She could see him smile as he opened the door and the light from the hallway illuminated his face. She heard him lock the door, trapping her inside, which curiously made her feel safer. She drank directly from one of the cartoons before closing her eyes and was fast asleep immediately.

Chapter XXXIX

Eric and his chartered jet were approaching Kyiv. He had just read Alicia's total retraction of her previous report and was not convinced. Among other things, it seemed to be more of a defensive response to what she had first submitted rather than a redaction of her report. He reread the short and rushed heads-up that had preceded this latest piece, which hastily informed him that she had been mistaken. *Well, I'll soon have clarification for myself in person*, he thought as the plane dipped in altitude and prepared for landing.

Eric was speedily checked through immigration and customs and was soon in a taxi and on his way to 11 Mirrors Design Hotel. Once there, despite the early hour, Alicia was not in her room. Neither was her roommate; Eric had been told to his surprise. This was not only odd but also worrisome to him since he hadn't been aware Alicia was sharing her room with someone else. However, Eric decided it was best not to admit this to the hotel staff. He thanked them and left.

It was too early to go to the embassy, so he decided to have a coffee across the street where he would have a view of the hotel's main entrance should Alicia return. While waiting for his order, he dialled Betty Unger's mobile number. She picked it up and told him she was on her way and would be at the embassy in half an hour.

Eric paid for his coffee as soon as it arrived. He drank it quicker than he would have liked due to his growing jitters. With no sign of Alicia, he called a taxi to meet Betty at the US Embassy.

Chapter XL

Alicia awoke to the sound of a key turning. At first, she didn't know where she was but when she saw the bartender in the doorway, her memory of the night before returned in a flash. She had slept surprisingly well and *oh boy* was she happy to see him. She was also thrilled about the fact that he was alone.

"Good morning, Alicia. Did you sleep well?"

"Good morning, Freddy. Yes, I slept like log. In fact, I just woke up this very moment."

"Good, I'll get you some coffee. Why don't you come out from over there and sit at the bar? It is only quarter to nine and there's nobody else here at this hour. The bar won't open until eleven o'clock."

Alicia was sitting sipping a wonderful dark strong coffee and suddenly had an idea. She reached into her jeans for a fifty-dollar bill pushed it across to Freddy and said, "Why don't you be a darling and fetch me a maid uniform?"

He took the bill and smiled at her as if understanding her plan precisely and promptly left. He was back in less than five minutes with the said uniform. Alicia unzipped and removed her jeans as Freddy spun around to give her privacy. She stuffed what little cash she had left into her new uniform as well as the neatly folded sheet of paper with Betty Unger's contact details. She lifted her long hair and swirled it gracefully underneath the hairnet Freddy had also managed to provide and was fully dressed as a maid. She finished by placing the little white hat on and smiled at Freddy as she asked, "How do I look?"

"Very well." It was all he could come up with.

"Thank you for everything, Freddy, goodbye," Alicia said before exiting the bar. She was careful to walk the stairs down to the lobby where she left the hotel through the staff entrance. Once outside, she looked around to quickly orientate herself to where she was. Soon she had her bearings and started walking with determination towards the Swedish embassy. She finally felt close to having her situation under control as she pressed the doorbell, fully aware of the camera above it. She heard a buzz and the reinforced steel door opened. She stepped inside and when the steel door closed behind her, she felt immediate relief. It was early and the consulate services had just started. Only two people were ahead of her as she grabbed a ticket. While waiting for her turn, she looked through the many pamphlets on a stand until she came upon one that had an almost blank page. She ripped out the page and folded it so that it was all white. Then she went up to the side of an unused service window and found a pen sitting there. Then she wrote:

My name is Alicia Byrne. I am a citizen of the USA. My life is in danger. Please call Betty Unger at the US Embassy.

When it was Alicia's turn, she stepped up to the window, said good morning, and handed over her ticket along with the note. The girl on the other side of the Plexiglas read the note after saying good morning. She looked up at Alicia with wide eyes but calmly asked her to wait. Then she got up and disappeared for a moment before sticking her head out through the door off to the side of all the desks and calling out to the security guard who was observing the waiting room. He promptly guided Alicia into a small meeting room. A few minutes later a woman, whom Alicia estimated to be in her early fifties, entered the room.

"Good morning. My name is Gudrun Eklund, and you must be Alicia Byrne. You seem to be in danger, is that so?"

"Hello, Gudrun. Yes, I am Alicia, and I am in grave danger. I have been held captive and only just managed to break free. Could you please contact Betty Unger at the US Embassy for me? I need you to tell her that I am a friend of Eric Holstein and that I need immediate protection."

"Alicia, would you by any chance have any kind of picture ID on you?"

"No, I don't. But please, believe me, I am Alicia Byrne, an American from New York, recently married to Adrian Franks."

"And you were held captive at the 11 Mirrors? Do you work there?" Gudrun inquired examining Alicia dressed up in her uniform.

"I was held captive at the hotel, yes but I don't work there. This is a disguise that I used to flee from the hotel."

"Well, you are certainly safe here. I know Mrs Unger. Do you want me to call and tell her that you are here with us and that you need them to come and pick you up?"

"Yes, please."

"But you don't know Mrs Unger, do you? Instead, you want me to tell her that you are a friend of a certain Eric Holstein, and that should suffice as far as Betty is concerned?"

"Yes, Eric gave me her name and contact details in case of an emergency. I believe they know each other well." Alicia was desperately hoping that this was indeed the case. "I have a valid passport which should be in room 408 at the 11 Mirrors Design Hotel. That is so long as my captors didn't take it."

"OK, I'll be right back," Gudrun said as she left.

Gudrun was back a few minutes later. "Your story checks out. I spoke with Betty, who is sending a car to pick you up. It should be no more than twenty minutes away. You see, the American embassy is a bit further out but it's lucky for you that we're so close. Meanwhile, you can wait here. Would you care for a cup of coffee?"

"Oh, yes, please. I had noticed the Swedish Embassy when I first arrived, well before my capture. I didn't just stumble upon it now; it was on the top of my list for my escape route. I don't even know where the US Embassy is."

"Well, you will soon." Gudrun returned shortly afterwards with Alicia's coffee and stretched out her hand to say goodbye before handing it over. "Best of luck to you, Alicia."

Chapter XLI

Eric hurried into Betty Unger's office at the embassy. They hugged and kissed each other's cheeks in a mad rush. "Now, Eric. Please sit down and make yourself comfortable. No need to worry about Alicia. She is being picked up as we speak and will be joining us soon."

"She is? How is that possible?" Eric looked totally stunned at first but then relief washed over him, and he burst out in happy laughter.

"You should never underestimate my abilities. Should you, Eric?" Betty asked with a mockingly grim face before laughing herself.

Indeed, an exhausted Alicia arrived only minutes later. She was still dressed in a maid's uniform as she stumbled into Betty's office. She looked startled at first but when she saw Eric, she started crying and rushed into his arms.

It was later discovered that all of Alicia's belongings had been left in the hotel room, except her computer and her passport. Olga had obviously also vanished.

"Whilst we don't deal in computers, we do provide passports," Betty exclaimed.

"I actually have most of my computer files uploaded to the cloud," Alicia said when she finally managed to speak.

After a shower at the embassy and changing into jeans and a jumper, Alicia was good to go. They shared their thanks and bid farewell to Betty, who also promised to extend Alicia's warmest regards to Gudrun at the Swedish Embassy. An armoured car drove Eric and Alicia to the airport where they boarded Eric's chartered plane. Once on the plane, Alicia finally felt able to relax and tell Eric everything, knowing she was safe, and her ordeal was finally over.

Chapter XLII

Several weeks had passed since Alicia's return to NYC, and Adrian had done wonders to help her heal and forget the ordeal in Kyiv. Her boss Stephen, on the other hand, had only contributed the question, repeatedly, over, and over again: "Who pays your salary? Ukraine or I?"

Miriam had contacted Alicia and told her that Jurjen was fine. His ordeal, which Alicia was now certain had been orchestrated to separate the two of them, had luckily left no permanent scars.

One day, Alicia had also received a call from Roland. He told her that Pavlov had requested she be reimbursed in full for all expenses related to her ill-fated trip. He was apparently most apologetic and had severed all ties with the Russian known as Igor. He failed to mention that this had been achieved largely as a result of the Kremlin's efforts.

Alicia's four-piece article about private adoptions in Ukraine was also finally finished. This very damaging piece, complete with details on the Russia collusion, was already in Eric's hands.

Chapter XLIII

Eric had finished reading Alicia's four-piece article. He had wanted to make some minor changes but had managed to refrain. *This is hers*, he reasoned. He emailed the work to his friend Bob Trumm, who called him an hour later from his office at NYT.

"Very good, Eric. No, it's excellent. And we would love to run it immediately. It just needs to get a 'sign-off' as you know."

"Glad to hear it, Bob. But I wonder, after the ordeal, Alicia went through, it would be nice if she could be properly compensated. Do you think you could pay her...I don't know, let's say fifty thousand?"

"With the new guidelines, it has become increasingly bureaucratic and complicated but sure. The easiest way would be to use a third party. Let me get back to you."

After hanging up, Bob immediately dialled another number.

Chapter XLIV

Beau Stewart stood in his private office overlooking Central Park. His penthouse view was, at least in his opinion, the best in all of New York City. Situated on the Upper Westside, Beau could see Central Park spread out like a carpet, surrounded by the most affluent parts of New York, its eastern and southern sides.

Beau was a fit man in his mid-fifties. He was neither handsome nor ugly. In fact, he was a man that somebody would find difficult to describe accurately if they had just met. This had served him well during his long career as a diplomat with mainly overseas postings involving low-level intelligence matters. He had never married and had no children. Although he was retired, he supplemented a nice pension with freelance work of the most varied kind. His attributes were his discretion and his trustworthiness. Many suspected he was homosexual, which he was but nobody cared. He always turned up at all official gatherings arm-in-arm with his best friend, Martha. She was a couple of years older than he was and acted as his confidant and surrogate wife.

Beau lived alone but this was to his liking. He didn't even have a pet. With so many contacts, and a reasonably busy life with NYC on his doorstep, Beau counted himself among the lucky ones; and he certainly enjoyed the freedom of his private space to withdraw into at the end of the day.

Checking his phone, he noticed he had a message to call Bob Trumm at the NYT, so he did. "Hello Bob," he said.

"Hi, Beau, thanks for calling back. I have a little favour to ask. A friend of mine has an article we want to publish, but he wants fifty grand. Could you set up a small bid so that I can justify the payment? You know, the usual suspects."

"Will the two posts do?"

"Yeah, that would be fine. You should contact Eric Holstein. He's staying at the Regency. Do you know him?"

"No, never heard of him. But I'll call him as soon as we hang up."

"Great. Nice talking to you, Beau."

This was neither a strange nor an unusual request. Beau would just stick ten thousand to the price for his service, which was pretty decent for a day's work. He immediately got a message containing Eric Holstein's number. He called him and they agreed to meet for breakfast at the Regency the following morning.

Chapter XLV

Beau entered the Regency the following morning. Already familiar with the hotel, he headed straight for the restaurant and enquired about Eric Holstein. He was immediately led to a corner table and shook hands with the handsome older man. Eric was as usual impeccably dressed in a charcoal grey suit and dark purple silk tie. Beau was also appropriately dressed in a blue checked sports blazer over a black cashmere turtleneck and light grey trousers.

Although breakfast at the Regency is a famous event, and a ritual for many of Wall Street's most powerful as a step on their way from the Upper East Side, both Eric and Beau only asked for two double espressos.

Eric asked Beau if he wanted to read the article. Beau declined, saying it was not necessary since he was just a convenient go-between. He did, however, give Eric a contract by which he, Beau, would acquire the rights to the article. He explained that the contract was standard and that he had left the consideration blank for Eric to fill in. He added that the sum mentioned by their mutual friend Bob Trumm was fifty thousand dollars. Eric confirmed this and filled in the amount. They both signed the contract with one copy; Beau handed Eric a cheque for the appropriate amount and Eric gave Beau an envelope containing the article.

"Do you know when it will be published?" Eric asked.

"My intervention should be over by tomorrow. As for when it will be published, that's something you need to ask Bob."

With that, both stood up, shook hands, and parted ways.

Chapter XLVI

Once back inside the walls of his penthouse after the meeting, Beau was again seated at his desk planning the day ahead. He felt a bit lazy and although he wasn't a heavy drinker, Beau decided he would enjoy a glass of scotch even though it wasn't yet noon. He poured himself a scotch over ice and fizzy water and started reading the article he had just purchased.

Half an hour later, he looked up from the article, uttered "What the heck?" and prepared another drink. What he had just read was dynamite. Although not mentioned by name, the article pointed at Pavlov Andreiko, the super-wealthy owner of Ukraine's sex industry, and its links to Russia and the Russian mob. The article might be worth fifty thousand American dollars where Beau was but he knew it would be worth much more than that over in Ukraine or Russia to somebody who wouldn't want to see it published at all. Thinking of the Russian mob sent chills down his spine but Pavlov, whom Beau actually knew from years back when he was briefly posted to Ukraine, was a different matter. Pavlov was foremost a businessman. However, Beau also had a problem in that he was supposedly acting for Bob and therefore not free to do whatever he pleased. "Delicate, most delicate," he whispered to himself as he sipped on his drink.

He checked his watch and calculated that it was early evening in Kyiv.

Finally, he dialled a number in Washington D.C. followed by to call to Ukraine. His third call was to Pavlov's personal private number.

"Hello?" Pavlov answered somewhat reluctantly since the number was private and therefore not displayed.

"Pavlov Andreiko, this is Beau Stewart calling from New York. We met many years ago when I was stationed at the US Embassy in Kyiv as Cultural Attaché. I hope you remember me."

Pavlov, who had a good memory of names, remembered the man who had been so helpful years ago and whom he had also helped by supplying him with male prostitutes. "But of course, Beau. What can I do for you?"

Beau explained to Pavlov as best as he could about the article and the fact that he had an opportunity to bid on purchasing the rights to the article. Pavlov listened carefully, painfully aware of where this was coming from but didn't say so. Before ending the call, Beau had agreed to immediately email the article to Pavlov and sit by waiting for his instructions. He didn't have to wait long for his phone to ring.

"Beau, this is Pavlov. Get that article for me, will you?"

"How high can I go with this bidding war?"

"Just get it for me. Go as high as five hundred thousand and keep me in the loop."

It was clear to Beau that this was not Pavlov's final offer, and so Beau had to speak with Eric Holstein again, urgently.

Chapter XLVII

Erik Holstein returned after lunch to the Regency. He had a message to urgently call Beau Stewart, which he did.

"Hello, Beau," he said. "What's so urgent?"

"Hello, Eric, and thanks for calling back. Do you have a minute?"

"Sure, Beau. Go ahead."

"Well, it turns out that I believe I can get you three times what I offered you for the article this morning from a different buyer."

"Wow, that sounds like a lot. Whilst I appreciate your honesty and your confidentiality, could you at least tell me if the prospective buyer is a reputable US news outlet?"

"What if it's not?"

"That puzzles me. Maybe we should meet?"

The two men agreed to meet again at the Regency in forty-five minutes. Beau quickly prepared a ham sandwich for lunch, which he washed down with a large cup of strong coffee to clear his head. He brushed his teeth and hurried downstairs, entered his Uber, and crossed Central Park.

Chapter XLVIII

Again, seated face-to-face in the bar at the Regency, Beau explained that after reading the article he had shown it to somebody who had come back to him very interested and willing to pay a much higher price. He, therefore, felt that it was his obligation to Eric but ultimately to the author, to share this vital piece of information.

Eric agreed and thanked him. "I am curious, though, as to why somebody should pay – what did you say? – three times as much. What's the catch?"

"I really couldn't tell you."

"Couldn't? Or won't?" Eric asked with a sly grin.

"Listen, Eric. You know I'm only a go-between and that it doesn't behove me to question motives. I'm only looking after my clients."

"Well, that sounds all good and well but I would be looking for some reassurance that the article will be published and circulated," Eric said.

"I am sorry for saying this, Eric, but shouldn't the author make that decision?"

"Yes, Beau, you are so right. I shall speak with her as soon as we're done here. Can you guarantee her one hundred and fifty thousand US dollars?"

"I can, maybe even two hundred thousand."

"Sounds extraordinary to me but let me check with Alicia and I will get back to you."

"Let me know as soon as possible. In the meantime, let's keep this between the three of us. I don't believe it's in anyone's interest to let Bob know. He'll only think we're trying to take the *NYT* for a ride."

"Agreed," Eric said. "Let me speak to Alicia and give you a call later today, alright?"

Beau thanked him and both gentlemen shook hands again before leaving.

Chapter XLIX

Eric knew exactly what to do next. "Hello, Darling Alicia, it's Eric. What are you and Adrian doing this evening?"

"Hi, Eric, what's up? I'm just about to pack up and head home from work."

"I was wondering if I could tempt you two with an invite to one of my favourite French restaurants. I want to have dinner with both of you this evening. There is something we need to discuss, and it is a matter of some urgency."

"Let me check with Adrian and I'll call you straight back."

Alicia spoke with Adrian, who told her he was going to be at work later than usual, before calling Eric back. "He told us to go ahead and have dinner without him. If he can, he'll join us for dessert. So where are we going?"

"La Goulue," Eric replied.

"But I thought it had closed?"

"Thankfully, it's reopened! I'm staying at the Regency, let's meet here?"

"Perfect. I'll be there in about twenty!" Alicia exclaimed excitedly.

Eric waited for Alicia in the lobby, and as soon as she arrived, they walked together the block and a half to the legendary restaurant, which had relocated to 61st street but was still near to where it had been previously. The new décor was amazing with stunning oak panels, matching wooden chairs, and brown leather booths. Hanging from the ceiling was a vast array of green foliage, which created a modern yet rustic feel that accompanied the French cuisine perfectly. Although it was not very different in the feel or style from before, both agreed it was a very smart upgrade.

After ordering, Alicia and Eric lifted their glasses. "Cheers!" They exclaimed both taking bigger gulps than usual and letting the wonderful French wine course through their bodies.

"Now to the topic of the evening." Eric became suddenly serious. "I have somebody, although I don't know whom, who is interested in paying at least one hundred and fifty thousand dollars, maybe two hundred thousand, for exclusive rights to your article."

"Seriously?" Alicia couldn't believe that amount. "What for?"

"That's the whole reason why I wanted to meet you in person because I don't know."

"So, I take it it's not *The New York Times*?"

"No, it definitely is not. They made a big deal about paying only fifty and even involved a middleman to make the offer," Eric confirmed.

"Could it be from somebody who wants the article buried rather than published?" she questioned.

"Funny you should ask that...I had precisely the same thought. But let's say you could get two hundred thousand for it, would it really matter?" he mused, allowing her to make her own decision without offering any opinion that might sway her decision. It was, after all, her article.

"Two hundred thousand? That's a lot of money. I would need to speak to Adrian and perhaps sleep on it. Is that alright?"

"They want to know by midnight, but I'll tell them you need more time. It is indeed a lot of money but who knows what will happen to your work," he cautioned.

"Exactly. I wouldn't want it to fall into the hands of someone who would bury it. People deserve to know," Alicia agreed.

"From the looks of it, Adrian won't be joining us. Let's call it a night and speak first thing tomorrow morning?" Eric suggested.

"Sounds good, and many thanks for a lovely dinner. So glad this place decided to reopen," Alicia said, sitting back and patting her full stomach contentedly.

Eric paid the bill and they walked back to his hotel together. Alicia hailed a cab and went home.

Chapter L

Pavlov was restless. Things were simply not progressing. It wasn't that he didn't trust Beau. He did. But he felt too removed from the negotiations. He decided to call Roland Thompson.

"Hello, Roland, it's me, Pavlov Andreiko."

"Mr Andreiko, what a pleasure! What can I do for you?"

Pavlov explained that he wanted Alicia Byrne's contact details. He also enquired as to how Roland was getting along with Alicia.

"Since you authorised me to refund all her expenses, I feel we are on very good terms. Why?" Roland said, aware he was stretching the truth here. In reality, he hadn't heard from Alicia since refunding her.

"Could you call her for me and tell her that I am very interested in making her a very interesting offer for an article she has written? I wish to call her directly if that's OK."

"Of course, will do," Roland replied, forcing himself to sound more confident than he felt.

"Roland, this is not only very important but also very urgent. Call me back as soon as you can."

Two hours later, and having heard nothing from Roland, Pavlov called him again. Roland admitted that he had tried to reach Alicia but had failed. He had left several voice messages for her to call him back but to no avail. Secretly, he was under the impression that she didn't want to talk to him.

"I see," Pavlov said. "Not to worry. Let's just drop it."

Now desperate, Pavlov placed a call to his attorney who promised to make contact with a top US law firm and call Pavlov back with a contact person and telephone number.

Chapter LI

Alicia and Adrian arrived home almost at the same time.

"Sorry, I couldn't make it to dinner, Darling," Adrian said as he hugged and kissed Alicia on her lips.

"Your loss. We went to Goulue," Alicia replied happily.

"Yeah, I heard that they reopened. How was it? I haven't been there."

"Fabulous, absolutely exquisite! Plus, I have some news. How does two hundred thousand dollars strike you? Well, at least one hundred and fifty."

"Tell me more!" Adrian eagerly responded.

Alicia filled Adrian in on the conversation she had had with Eric, and they ended up discussing why somebody might want to pay more to bury an article than somebody else who would be willing to pay to have it published. They also discussed how a portion of that money could be spent booking a restaurant for their wedding reception since their living space, although two apartments combined, would only be able to accommodate thirty-five people tops. They expected the number of people attending the church ceremony would be about eighty and they needed to know the numbers and venue for the reception since they hoped to send the wedding invitations out the following week. They also discussed how the extra money could be spent on flying Miriam and Jurjen out to attend the wedding, rather than offering to go Dutch with them as they had previously planned.

Chapter LII

Leighton Boss, the managing partner of the law firm Sterling & Boss, had just hung up the phone with Pavlov Andreiko. His instructions were clear. He was to contact a Mrs Alicia Byrne and offer her the staggering sum of three hundred thousand American dollars for exclusive rights to her article on Ukrainian adoptions, together with the rights to any subsequent material related to the subject, should she produce it. He was to contact her at her workplace, Bowen & Hughes. He promptly did as instructed.

"Hello, Mrs Byrne. My name is Leighton Boss of Sterling & Boss. I am calling you to present you with a very attractive cash offer in lieu of an article you recently wrote, and I believe…"

"Sorry for interrupting you, Mr Boss, but I must refer you to Eric Holstein. He is acting on my behalf in this matter." She gave him Eric's phone number and excused herself.

She didn't want to hear me out at all, Leighton thought disappointedly to himself. *Better try this Eric Holstein fellow then.* He called and tried again. "Hello, Mr Holstein, my name is Leighton Boss of Sterling & Boss. I just spoke with Alicia Byrne about an article of hers and she referred me to you."

"Hello, Leighton. Please, call me Eric."

"Eric, I have an offer on behalf of one of our overseas clients who are interested in exclusive rights to Alicia's article on Ukrainian adoptions. The client also wants any further writings of hers on this subject or anything related to it. The offer is three hundred thousand dollars."

"That's a kind offer, Leighton. What kind of timeline am I working with here?"

"If you could let me know by this evening, that would be great."

"I'll take that to mean that your offer expires by midnight tonight, New York time?" Eric confirmed.

"Very well. Goodbye for now."

After hanging up with Leighton, Eric immediately called Bob at the NYT. Eric put all the cards on the table and Bob just said that the offer was ridiculous and if real, meant that somebody wanted to pay an exorbitant price to prevent the article from being published. Eric agreed but pleaded with his friend. "Bob, help me out. What can I do except tell her to take the money and forget the story?"

"Well, you didn't hear this from me but over at *The Post*, they have a scheme by which they call in financial favours from outside donors for special situations. The person to contact is Louis Pallet. Remember that you didn't hear it from me."

Eric thanked Bob and immediately called Louis at *The New York Post*. He explained the situation and sent over the article by email. Louis confirmed that *The Post* was interested and that he would call back early evening.

True to his word, Louis called back at half six. "We've got a grand total of one-six-five!"

Eric was silent at first, thinking about what Alicia would want before finally agreeing, "We have ourselves a deal, Louis. We have ourselves a deal."

During his silence, Eric had decided to pitch in with thirty-five thousand of his own to make it an even two hundred thousand for Alicia. After all, he had received a full refund of what he had given to her as an advance for her Ukraine adoption project. Plus, it was Alicia.

Chapter LIII

Bob was sitting in the Chief Editor's office at the *NYT*. Both men were drinking coffee from paper cups. They were looking at today's edition of *The New York Post*. The cover, at the bottom left corner, read 'Russian Babies Adopted through Ukraine' (Story on page 5)'.

Flipping to it, Alicia Byrne's article, the first part of four, was completely re-written in an investigative and sensationalistic style that the *NYT* did not possess. It promised the second part in tomorrow's edition.

"But I thought that we were to run this story, Bob. What happened?" The Chief Editor asked.

"We were outbid."

"Outbid? That simple? Well, was it by a lot?"

"Yes, by a lot. A whole lot of money," Bob replied, knowing the editor would be annoyed to have missed out to their rivals but confident in the fact that the *NYT* would never have paid more than their original offer.

"Are we talking hundreds of thousands?"

"Yes, we are."

"What the fuck! We're *The New York Times*, for fuck's sake! And who the fuck are they, *The Post*?" He pronounced the word post as if it were a grotesque indecent act.

Both men, although undecided on what to do next, stood up and grabbed their unfinished coffees. They stormed out of the office and left behind what they reasoned was an insignificant episode in the glorious history of *The New York Times*.

At the same time, Alicia was crying tears of joy and jumping up and down in the arms of Eric, who had made a point of personally delivering a cheque for two hundred thousand to her workplace. Stephen Hughes, the managing partner of Bowen & Hughes, looked on, mystified at the scene, through the glass wall of his corner office.

"But this cheque is your personal cheque, Eric. This isn't from *The Post*," Alicia finally managed to say after trying to rub her cheeks dry of her tears.

"That's because *The Post* gave me five different cheques, so I had them deposited in my account so that I could give you one big one." Although this was technically true, he failed to mention that those five cheques didn't quite add up to the final sum he had handed her. He decided to leave out that small detail.

Chapter LIV

Pavlov was seated outside despite the sub-zero temperature. He wore a warm fur coat but left it undone and wore nothing on his head. Two efficient gas burners on each side of the small table kept the café's outdoor patio decently warm. The early evening was pitch black as usual in Kyiv in the month of November. On the table in front of him were black coffee and a glass of brandy. He puffed on a cigar as he contemplated recent events.

It had all started with Alicia Byrne's ill-fated trip to Kyiv under the false pretence of wanting to adopt. Or had it started much earlier when that bastard Igor had visited and proposed the whole adoption scheme in the first place? Whatever the case, it was finally, and thankfully, in the past. *But not without a hefty price tag*, Pavlov thought to himself. He had finally had to call on help from Moscow. As a result, a large contingent of people had descended on Kyiv to assist with the reorganisation of his financial affairs. Led by the Russians, the team also included a small Ukrainian contingency, the vast majority consisted of bankers and lawyers from West European countries though. The result was twofold. Firstly, it had cost him a small fortune, and secondly, he no longer had any American cash, other than what was floating around in his business outlets.

Pavlov's business empire now consisted mainly of companies based in Cyprus with subsidiaries all over Europe, the Middle East, and Hong Kong. Financial assets were in physical gold held in Switzerland and London, money deposits, and other financial instruments denominated in euros, Swiss francs, pounds, yuan, and even Bitcoin.

Pavlov's name was rumoured to be on the next Magnitsky Act list. Although this was by no means difficult to confirm, Pavlov just couldn't be bothered. He had no American financial holdings or assets anymore, nor any dealings with any of that country's institutions. Furthermore, Pavlov had no interest whatsoever in visiting the land as he had never been before, nor wanted to.

He waved to the waiter to settle his bill and gulped down the last of the brandy. After paying he stood up and made his way to the black Mercedes where Andre was patiently awaiting him.

Chapter LV

Alicia had tackled many things in her almost forty years but she had yet to plan a wedding. You could say that she was nervous although the right word perhaps might be anxious. She wanted everything to be perfect. She was, after all, legally married to Adrian already, so she had no nerves about that side of things. *I just want my dream wedding,* she thought. *I can't ask Elisabeth for help. No, my dream wedding is very different from hers; something less extravagant and modern but still tasteful and classic.*

First things first, she needed to send out the invites. The invitations were simple; plain white with gold silhouetted grey letters for the church ceremony. A little card with the details of the restaurant was to be included in just over half of the envelopes. She thought that most of the nearly ninety guests would turn up for the church, and they had made reservations for 52 at the nearby 'Gabriels' for dinner afterwards. They had been unanimous in their decision to invite Miriam and Jurjen, complete with airfare and hotel accommodation. After all, they were victims as well as Alicia in her quest to find the truth behind the babies from Ukraine. Her thoughts were suddenly interrupted.

"Mrs Byrne, I assume." Alicia startled from her reverie, looked up to see her boss, Stephen, leaning against her open office doorframe. Alicia decided to shrug off Stephen's comment. *So typical of him*, she thought.

"Oh Stephen, you scared me," she said, truthfully.

"Am I interrupting something?" Stephen quipped in a jolly and somewhat annoying way as he looked down at the invitations spread out on her desk.

"Not at all," she replied, trying to sound more casual than she felt as she steadied herself.

"Busy planning, are we?" Stephen rather obviously pointed out.

"Well, it is once in a lifetime," she protested.

"Let's hope so." His answer sounded like an old cliché, and he immediately wished that he had chosen to say something different.

"Of course." Alicia immediately understood what he meant but men just don't understand that however many times a woman marries, she will never go through with planning a wedding quite the same twice. Then, she had a thought, *I'll involve him, it might be the best way out of this situation.*

"Why don't you have a look, Stephen," she said, showing him the invitation card and accompanying restaurant card while explaining the numbers involved. What she failed to mention was the twenty-five or so intimate friends that she and Adrian expected to follow them after dinner to their joint apartments for a little after-wedding bash. He wouldn't be invited to that part of the day. She made sure she explained to him that the seating at the restaurant was 'free' except for Adrian's and her table which was reserved for only family. She couldn't think of anything worse than her boss trying to sit at their table.

"You have obviously given a lot of thought to this; I am positive that everything will go as planned," he replied, satisfied that he had been invited to the wedding, having previously felt a bit miffed to be left out; he had always had a soft spot for Alicia, not that he'd admit that.

"Thank you, Stephen!" she replied feeling relieved that he seemed happy. "And I haven't forgotten this month's numbers which I shall bring to you in ten." She made sure she mentioned this, so he knew she had actually been working as well as wedding planning.

"Good. Then I shall excuse myself." He swung around and walked back to his corner office.

Chapter LVI

Alicia was back at her desk after having gone through the month's billing accounts with Stephen as promised. However, she couldn't help herself and went straight back to the wedding preparations.

The Church of St Paul the Apostle was, of course, her choice. Both majestic and beautiful, she really couldn't think of a more wonderful place for their official wedding ceremony. As it turned out, their previous wedding certificate from the state of Virginia, while legal in nature, provided no hindrance whatsoever for 'the real thing'. The restaurant, Gabriels, on the other hand, had been chosen by Adrian and his father but she had supposedly had the final say after a dinner there which Adrian's mother had also attended. She loved both the food and the atmosphere and was particularly impressed with the veggie alternative menu, which both Adrian and she deemed necessary. *I am so blessed,* she mused.

Alicia was again interrupted, this time by her buzzing mobile.

"Hello."

"Hi, Alicia, it's Eric."

"Well, hey there," she replied happily.

"How are the wedding preparations going?"

"I am just putting some final touches on them," she said excitedly.

"I assume that I am allowed to bring somebody?" he enquired.

"But of course, Eric. Who is she?" Alicia couldn't hide the excitement.

"It is actually a 'he', and you've never met him."

"Sounds very intriguing to me," Alicia said curiously, she had thought Eric preferred the company of women and wondered if perhaps she had been wrong in this assumption.

"It should be." Eric chuckled enjoying Alicia's obvious confusion. "He is somebody who you've never met but who was very instrumental in getting your big payment for your articles in the *New York Post*."

"So, he works for *The Post*?" she enquired.

"No, he does not. The story is far more interesting than that."

"Now I really am curious. You must fill me in so that I know what to say when I meet him. What's his name?" Alicia rapidly fired off, keen to hear more.

"Not so fast. What about lunch? Le Colonial at one? I'll give you the whole story." Eric assured her.

"Love to! One it is," she said, before hanging up the phone.

Once seated at their familiar table at Le Colonial, while munching the numerous and delicious small dishes, Eric explained in detail how Beau Stewart's intervention had led to the stakes being raised in terms of her article. Alicia listened to the story with fascination, and it was confirmed that Pavlov's efforts in not having her story published was the key to the price she eventually managed to get, thanks really to Eric and his ultimate contact at *The Post*. But of course, one shouldn't downplay Beau's role in unravelling the events.

Chapter LVII

At the same time, almost five thousand miles away, Igor Kovalenko sat in a bar that can only be described as the exact opposite of the one Alicia and Eric were currently in. The air hanging over the bar was heavy with smoke, and the lights gave away a brown, yellowish light as if stained by nicotine. The sparse furnishings were worn and the three pool tables were visibly damaged; no music was playing. For lack of better words, the place was shabby at best and, quite frankly, a dump. No more than fifteen guests were present, which was average for a Tuesday night or any other night for that matter. Two ill-dressed men were playing a game of chess at one of the tables. Nobody was watching, which was just as well since their playing skills did not live up to anything resembling Russian chess masters. Their concentration was instead focused on negotiating a 'contract'. The negotiation was more a haggle over money, and not a lot of money at that; life was not an expensive commodity in this lawless part of the world on the outskirts of Moscow. Having concluded their negotiations but not their chess game, the two-headed for the bar register. Igor, who had watched the two men for a short while with uninterested eyes, now attended to their business. At their instructions, he opened his laptop and made a few entries. Once done, he flipped the screen over, and the two men nodded in agreement. He made a quick calculation on his

Casio calculator and showed it to the men. One of them handed over a bunch of crumpled dollar bills to Igor, which he took and placed in a steel box below the counter. He also handed both men a glass of vodka, apparently 'on the house' as no further cash exchanged hands. The two men acknowledged each other with a nod, said, "Na zdorovie" (often mispronounced by foreigners as *nostrovia*, meaning 'cheers' in Russian), and drained their glasses, before exiting the bar.

Igor returned his attention to the other guests who were scattered about the place. Beside him was his only employee, a woman in her forties with lots of makeup but which could hardly be detected in the low light of the establishment. From previously having been a powerful, and upcoming mobster within the 'Bratva', this was now Igor's life, at least for the moment. He cursed to himself in an almost inaudible voice. Truthfully though, Igor was thankful to be alive, and not in a labour camp somewhere in Siberia from where there was no return. He knew very well, however, that first he had to do his time here, serving low-level drunks and petty criminals.

"Fucking Kyiv, fucking Alicia Byrne, and fucking Pavlov," he muttered to himself. One day soon he would be back from hiding and working with the Bratva again. Then he would make them all pay, starting with that bitch Alicia Byrne, he thought to himself.

Chapter LVIII

Alicia and Adrian's wedding ceremony was in the Church of St Paul the Apostle, a Roman Catholic Church located on the West Side. Alicia and Adrian had fallen in love with the late Victorian gothic revival style with its marbled floors and pillars, high ceilings, and rich history. The ceremony was to take place at four pm that day, followed by a champagne reception and dinner for 52 at Gabriel's, a delicious and upmarket Italian restaurant that was only a five-minute cab ride (or ten-minute walk) away. Following that, twenty-five of their closest friends and family would head back for an after-party at Alicia and Adrian's combined apartments to celebrate into the small hours while nibbling on canapés.

Around three-thirty pm the guests begin to arrive, slowly filling up the pews and greeting each other warmly. Adrian and his groomsmen, who are all wearing perfectly tailored navy-blue three-piece suits and classic cream ties, are already there welcoming the guests and directing them to their seats. Adrian spots Miriam and Jurjen awkwardly hovering near the entrance, not knowing anyone other than the bride and groom. He strides over to greet them and finally meet them in person before sitting them next to Eric and Beau who have already arrived. The couple gratefully take their seats and begin happily chatting with the effervescent duo, quickly becoming firm friends, as Alicia knew they would.

Chapter LIX

Meanwhile, as Adrian is already at the church distracted from his nerves by his task of meeting and greeting, Alicia is finishing getting ready to head to the church herself. As she gets into the traditional old-fashioned Bentley wedding car they have hired for the event, Alicia breathes a sigh of relief that she will have five minutes of peace in the car; grateful that only her dad is travelling with her to the church while her bridesmaids and mother follow in their own car behind.

"You look breathtaking, sweetheart." Her dad remarks proudly with tears in his eyes.

"Thanks, Dad. I know." Alicia giggled, trying to hide her nerves with a joke. Although, she knows she *does* look stunning in her Versace dress and chic bun with tendrils that frame her perfectly natural and subtle makeup. She fell in love with the classy and traditional gown as soon as she saw it and knew it was 'the one'. The dress was fitted at the waist with a flowing bottom half, a long train, and long lace sleeves. In her shaking hands, she held a bouquet of simple cream roses.

Not falling for her false bravado, her dad took her hand in his and said, "Your mother and I love you very much. Adrian is perfect for you but it's natural to have some wedding day jitters."

"Thanks, Dad. I know," Alicia replied, this time entirely sincerely and relieved to know her dad felt, as she did, that she was marrying the right man.

Chapter LX

Alicia took a deep breath and readied herself as they stood outside the large wooden doors at the entrance of the church. In front of her stood Barbara, Elisabeth, and her sister all looking beautiful in their classic yet simple cream silk bridesmaid's dresses.

Unsurprisingly, all three bridesmaids had been shocked at Alicia's decision that they should be in cream, remarking that "only the bride should wear cream or white!" However, Alicia had been adamant that she wanted the traditional cream bridesmaid's dresses. To which Barbara had replied, in her usual droll way, "Well, if the royals in England do it, why not us? So long as no one expects me to be virginal!"

Chapter LXI

Much later, after that day, guests would recall having seen a tall, muscular man in an all-black suit, shirt, and tie also waiting outside of the church that morning as they entered. The man stood off to the side away from everyone else leaning against a black Audi. Presumably, they thought, because he was smoking a cigarette, or perhaps didn't know many others there, or perhaps he was even someone's driver waiting outside for them. The man did not speak to anyone, nor did anyone recognise him.

Alicia and the bridal party did not notice the man intently watching them from afar as they anxiously awaited their entrance.

Chapter LXII

Once the bridesmaids had made their way inside, Alicia and her dad were ready to go in as well. Alicia had never been more grateful to have her dad by her side and she knew he felt the same.

Walking down the aisle, Alicia could feel the eyes of her guests on her but all she could see was Adrian. The expression on his face was one of pure love and adoration and, at that moment, Alicia knew he was the only man she could ever love for the rest of her life and that they would grow old together.

Having been handed over by her father, Alicia looked at Adrian and felt a moment of pure unadulterated happiness and excitement. She also glanced at the Priest, their eyes quickly locked in a moment of mutual approval, before turning her attention to the crowd of loved ones that had made it to the ceremony. Her inspection revealed a multi-coloured tapestry of hair, suits, neckties, and dresses but she couldn't make out any faces. That is, apart from, somewhat unexpectedly, her mother's, whose usual cool indifference towards her was forgotten in that moment; for her mother was crying. Alicia rarely saw her mother cry, and especially not due to pride and love for her.

How beautiful this is, she thought. It is all about me, no us...no, it is much more, and you are my witnesses! She suddenly felt the need for a glass of whiskey to stabilise herself. She cleared her throat as she and Adrian begin to repeat their vows back at the Priest.

Chapter LXIII

"I now pronounce you husband and wife. You may kiss the bride."

"You don't have to ask me twice!" Adrian replied, winking cheekily at the shocked Priest before scooping Alicia into a long kiss to the sounds of the congregation's cheers.

Alicia beams up at her new husband before taking his hand and turning to face their friends and family, ready to head back down the aisle as husband and wife. As she looks out into the sea of smiling faces, she spots a man she doesn't recognise striding down the aisle towards them. *How odd,* she thinks, *perhaps it is Eric's plus one, Beau. But why would he be trying to introduce himself now of all times, and he's certainly not what I expected.*

The man who is of an incredibly large, intimidating, and muscular stature continues his approach, reaching into his jacket pocket as he does so. Unnoticed by the crowd of well-wishers who are still all looking at the happy couple.

Adrian has also noticed the man but unlike Alicia, he knows this man cannot be a guest. This is why when he sees the man reaching into his pocket, he senses the danger, and without thinking, jumps in front of his bride.

Chapter LXIV

Alicia is still pondering the strange man as Adrian abruptly jumps in front of her knocking her backwards slightly. She hears a loud bang, *a car backfiring perhaps,* she thinks, before noticing the man is now running back down the aisle away from them.

Chapter LXV

The horror of what has just happened doesn't seem to be sinking in, as though her brain won't allow it. She hears distraught animalistic screams, and it is only when she sees her dad and Eric running towards her from out of the horrified crowd that she realises the screams are her own.

Chapter LXVI

Adrian's blood is staining her white gown crimson as she cradles him in her arms, and all she can think is, *please God, don't let him die. Not without knowing I'm pregnant. Not without meeting our child.*

But there's too much blood.
No, the paramedics will be here soon. He must live.
He has to.

Chapter LXVII

Alicia sits, still in her bloodstained wedding gown, in the back of the ambulance clinging onto Adrian's hand like a drowning woman as the paramedics frantically work on trying to stem the flow of blood to stabilise him.

"We're losing him!" They shout, reaching for the defibrillator.

The young paramedic with the kind eyes who had smiled so sadly at her as she insisted on riding with Adrian, is now fully intent on saving Adrian.

"We have a pulse but it's a faint one," he says as they race towards the hospital. All the while Alicia is continuing her internal mantra, *please God, don't let him die.*

Chapter LXVIII

Below is an extract from the front page of the *New York Post*.

Heroic Bridegroom Shot at the Alter While Shielding Bride

The wedding day of Adrian Franks and Alicia Byrne ended in tragedy yesterday when an unidentified assailant shot and grievously injured the groom. Alicia Byrne, our very own correspondent, who recently wrote the four-part expose on the illegal adoption of Russian babies through Ukraine, is suggested to have been the intended target. While police have yet to confirm this, inside sources have informed us that Mr Franks was shot when he heroically stepped in front of his bride to protect her from the bullet that was meant for her. Police have yet to confirm a suspect but state that they are pursuing several leads. It is said that Mrs Byrne was uninjured and has not left her new husband's side, while he remains in critical condition. The shooting occurred...
(Continued on page 5)

Chapter LXIX

Alicia sits in the church pew dressed in all black including a black veil she wears to shield her red-rimmed eyes, a macabre reminder of her wedding veil. Her hands are clenched in prayer as she watches the only man she ever truly loved get carried down the church aisle in a coffin, the same aisle that only a month ago they had stood at the top of and vowed to love each other "until death do us part". *If only that vow hadn't come to fruition so soon.* She thinks, aching at the thought of all she had lost, and all that her unborn child would never have. *How would her life be raising a child as a single mother in her forties? How would her child feel, growing up without a father?*

Alicia tries not to think about when they were last here, about the blood, or the man, who is still at large, and why he wanted to kill her. She can't help wondering, *am I still in danger? Will I and my unborn child be next?* She clutches her stomach in sheer horror at the thought of it. No, she cannot think like this. Today she is here to say goodbye to Adrian. *But I will never forget him, and our child shall grow up hearing all about how wonderful their father was.* She thinks, looking down and whispering to the life growing inside of her, her last remaining connection with the man she loved.

"Darling, we are here to say goodbye to your father, the greatest man I have ever known, who died to save us both, and who, sadly, you will never meet."

THE END

CPSIA information can be obtained
at www.ICGtesting.com
Printed in the USA
BVHW030828071222
653642BV00011B/146